EDITOR: Maryanne Blacker
FOOD EDITOR: Pamela Clark

• • •

DESIGNER: Robbylee Phelan

• • •

DEPUTY FOOD EDITOR: Barbara Northwood
HOME ECONOMISTS: Jane Ash, Tikki Durant,
Sue Hipwell, Karen Maughan, Voula Mantzouridis,
Louise Patniotis, Kathy Wharton
EDITORIAL ASSISTANT: Elizabeth Gray
KITCHEN ASSISTANT: Amy Wong

• • •

PHOTOGRAPHERS: Kevin Brown, Robert Clark,
Paul Clarke, Andre Martin, Robert Taylor,
Justine Kerrigan, Georgia Moxham
STYLISTS: Rosemary De Santis, Carolyn Fienberg,
Michelle Gorry, Jacqui Hing, Anna Phillips,
Jenny Wells, Jon Allen

• • •

HOME LIBRARY EDITORIAL COORDINATOR:
Fiona Nicholas

• • •

ACP PUBLISHER: Richard Walsh
ACP DEPUTY PUBLISHER: Nick Chan

• • •

Produced by The Australian Women's Weekly
Home Library. Typeset by ACP Colour Graphics Pty Ltd,
Sydney. Printed by Times Printers Pte Ltd, Singapore.
Published by ACP Publishing, 54 Park Street Sydney.
AUSTRALIA: Distributed by Network Distribution Company,
54 Park Street Sydney, (02) 282 8777.
♦ UNITED KINGDOM: Distributed in the U.K. by ACP
Publishing (UK) Ltd, 20 Galowhill Rd, Brackmills,
Northampton NN4 OEE (0604) 760 456.
♦ CANADA: Distributed in Canada by Whitecap Books Ltd,
86 West 3rd St, North Vancouver V7P 3J6 (604) 980 9852.
♦ NEW ZEALAND: Distributed by Netlink Distribution
Company, 17B Hargreaves St, Level 5, College Hill,
Auckland 1 (9) 302 7616.
♦ SOUTH AFRICA: Distributed in South Africa by Intermag,
PO Box 57394, Springfield 2137 (011) 493 3200.

• • •

• • •

Vegetarian Cooking
Includes index.
ISBN 0 949892 56 4
1.Vegetarian cookery. 1. Title: Australian
Women's Weekly Home Library
641.5636

• • •

FRONT COVER: Clockwise, from top: Avocado and
Garbanzo Salad, page 17; Witlof and Fruit Salad, page 64;
Fruity Seasoned Peppers, page 46.
Table, quilt, plates & board: The Country Trader;
wooden bowls: Gallery Nomad; basket: Corso de Fiori,
cabinet: Gregory Ford Antiques.
OPPOSITE: From top: Sunflower Fruit Salad; Brown Sugar
Meringues with Carob Cream, page 76.
BACK COVER: Clockwise from top left: Apricot Spiral
Teacake, page 86. Minted Parsely Salad, page 72. Spicy
vegetable in Crispy Baskets, page 32, Snow Pea, Apple and
Nut Salad, page 72.
·le, quilt, plates & whisk: The Country Trader; wooden bowls:
Gallery Nomad; cabinet: Gregory Ford Antiques.

VEGETARIAN COOKING

If you enjoy eating well, you will enjoy this book. We have taken a middle-of-the-road point of view, and based our recipes on vegetarian principles without being too strict. We naturally did not use meat, but included eggs and dairy products in many recipes. You can also introduce your family to vegetarianism by using our recipes as accompaniments to meat, chicken or fish. If embarking on vegetarianism as a way of life, you need to research and understand foods to be sure your meals are balanced. We have used some ingredients that may be new to you; these are described in the glossary. And we show you how to prepare yoghurt, bean sprouts, peanut butter, mayonnaise, soy milk and cottage cheese. Our recipes contain no salt. Instead, we used vegetable stock cubes and vegetable stock paste to boost flavours; these can be omitted, if you prefer.

Pamela Clark
FOOD EDITOR

P9-CQX-173

BRITISH & NORTH AMERICAN READERS: Please note that Australian cup
and spoon measurements are metric. A quick conversion guide appears on page 128.

Soups

Vegetables are the natural basis of these delicious and popular soups. They adapt without fuss to all types, ranging from hearty family fare to stylish starters for a dinner party. Some of our recipes reflect influences from international cuisines; most are subtly enhanced by readily-available herbs.

VEGETABLE AND BARLEY SOUP

Soup can be made several hours ahead; keep, covered, in refrigerator. Recipe unsuitable to freeze.

½ cup pearl barley
3 cups water
1 tablespoon oil
1 medium onion, chopped
1 clove garlic, crushed
2 medium carrots, chopped
1 medium potato, chopped
1 stick celery, chopped
425g can tomatoes
1 large vegetable stock cube, crumbled
2 tablespoons chopped fresh parsley

Soak barley in the water overnight. Heat oil in large saucepan, add onion and garlic, stir over medium heat for about 2 minutes (or microwave on HIGH for about 3 minutes) or until onion is soft. Add carrots, potato, celery, undrained crushed tomatoes, stock cube, undrained barley and water mixture. Bring to boil, reduce heat, cover, simmer for about 15 minutes (or microwave on HIGH for about 15 minutes) or until vegetables are tender. Stir in the parsley just before serving.
Serves 4.

CHICK PEA AND LEEK SOUP

Soup can be made a day ahead; keep, covered, in refrigerator. Recipe unsuitable to freeze or microwave.

2 cups (375g) dried chick peas
1 medium leek, sliced
2 medium onions, sliced
2 bay leaves
2 teaspoons chopped fresh thyme
2 teaspoons chopped fresh marjoram
1½ tablespoons Vecon
2 litres (8 cups) water
1½ cups shredded cabbage
125g broccoli, chopped
2 sticks celery, sliced

Soak peas in water overnight, drain. Combine leek, onions, bay leaves, herbs, Vecon, water and chick peas in large saucepan. Bring to boil, reduce heat, cover, simmer for 1 hour. Add cabbage, broccoli and celery, cover, simmer for about 15 minutes or until vegetables are tender. Remove bay leaves before serving.
Serves 6.

GREEN BEAN AND COCONUT CREAM SOUP

Prepare soup close to serving time. This recipe is not suitable to freeze or microwave.

1 medium carrot
30g butter
2 teaspoons chopped fresh lemon grass
2 cloves garlic, crushed
1 teaspoon grated fresh ginger
1 teaspoon ground turmeric
2 teaspoons ground coriander
2 fresh green chillies, chopped
2 green shallots, chopped
½ cup chopped green beans
2 x 400ml cans coconut cream
½ large vegetable stock cube, crumbled
2 cups (125g) bean sprouts
2 tablespoons chopped fresh coriander

Cut carrot into fine strips. Melt butter in large saucepan, add lemon grass, garlic and ginger, stir over medium heat for 1 minute. Add turmeric and ground coriander, stir over heat further 1 minute. Add carrot, chillies, shallots, beans, coconut cream and stock cube, mix well. Bring to boil, reduce heat, simmer, uncovered, for 5 minutes. Stir in bean sprouts and fresh coriander.
Serves 4.

From top: Chick Pea and Leek Soup; Vegetable and Barley Soup.

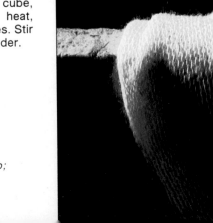

CURRIED BEAN AND MUSHROOM SOUP

Soup can be prepared 3 days ahead; keep, covered, in refrigerator. Soup can be frozen for 2 months.

½ cup dried red kidney beans
½ cup dried black-eyed beans
30g butter
1 small leek, sliced
1 small carrot, chopped
125g baby mushrooms, sliced
1 teaspoon curry powder
410g can tomatoes
3 cups water
1 large vegetable stock cube, crumbled
1 tablespoon chopped fresh parsley

Place beans in large bowl, cover with boiling water, stand for 1 hour, drain. Cook beans in large saucepan of boiling water for about 25 minutes (or microwave on HIGH for about 20 minutes) or until tender; drain.

Melt butter in large saucepan, add leek, stir over medium heat for about 5 minutes (or microwave on HIGH for about 3 minutes) or until leek is soft. Add carrot, mushrooms and curry powder, stir over medium heat for about 1 minute (or microwave on HIGH for 1 minute).

Stir in beans, undrained crushed tomatoes, water and stock cube. Bring to boil, reduce heat, cover, simmer for about 35 minutes (or microwave on HIGH for about 25 minutes) or until beans are tender. Stir in parsley.

Serves 6.

KUMARA AND LENTIL SOUP

Soup can be made 3 days ahead; keep, covered, in refrigerator. Soup can be frozen for 2 months.

2 teaspoons oil
1 small onion, chopped
1 medium (300g) kumara, chopped
1 cup red lentils
1 large vegetable stock cube, crumbled
3 cups water

Heat oil in large saucepan, add onion, stir over medium heat for about 2 minutes (or microwave on HIGH for about 2 minutes) or until onion is soft. Add remaining ingredients, bring to boil, reduce heat, cover, simmer for about 20 minutes (or microwave on HIGH for about 10 minutes) or until kumara is soft. Blend mixture in several batches until smooth, return to saucepan, reheat before serving. Serve with plain yoghurt, if desired.

Serves 4.

ABOVE: Green Bean and Coconut Cream Soup. RIGHT: From top: Curried Bean and Mushroom Soup; Cream of Broccoli Soup.

Cabinet: Strange Cargo Antiques

CREAM OF BROCCOLI SOUP

Soup can be made a day ahead; keep, covered, in refrigerator. Recipe unsuitable to freeze.

90g butter
2 medium onions, chopped
½ cup wholemeal plain flour
1½ litres (6 cups) water
1 tablespoon Vecon
750g broccoli, chopped
1 medium tomato, chopped
1 teaspoon chopped fresh thyme
½ teaspoon chopped fresh rosemary
¼ teaspoon ground nutmeg
1 tablespoon lemon juice
1 cup milk
¾ cup plain yoghurt

Melt butter in large saucepan, add onions, stir over medium heat for about 3 minutes (or microwave on HIGH for about 4 minutes) or until onions are soft. Stir in flour, stir over medium heat for 1 minute (or microwave on HIGH for 1 minute). Gradually stir in water, Vecon, broccoli, tomato, thyme, rosemary, nutmeg and juice, bring to boil, stirring. Reduce heat, cover, simmer for about 15 minutes (or microwave on HIGH for about 20 minutes) or until broccoli is tender. Blend mixture in several batches until smooth, add milk and yoghurt, return to saucepan, reheat without boiling.

Serves 6.

TOMATO AND PASTA SOUP

We used wholemeal casarecce pasta for this recipe. Soup can be made a day ahead; keep, covered, in refrigerator. This recipe is unsuitable to freeze.

15g butter
1 medium onion, chopped
1 clove garlic, crushed
2 cups water
1 large vegetable stock cube, crumbled
5 medium (500g) tomatoes, chopped
2 tablespoons tomato paste
1 tablespoon chopped fresh basil
90g wholemeal pasta

Melt butter in large saucepan, add onion and garlic, stir over medium heat for about 2 minutes (or microwave on HIGH for about 3 minutes) or until onion is soft. Add water, stock cube, tomatoes, paste and basil. Bring to boil, reduce heat, cover, simmer for about 20 minutes (or microwave on HIGH for about 20 minutes) or until tomatoes are cooked.

Add pasta gradually to large saucepan of boiling water, boil, uncovered, for about 8 minutes or until pasta is tender, drain. Blend or process tomato mixture in several batches until smooth, stir in pasta.

Serves 4.

CHUNKY VEGETABLE SOUP

Soup can be made a day ahead; keep, covered, in refrigerator. This recipe is unsuitable to freeze.

45g butter
1 medium leek, sliced
¼ cup white plain flour
1¼ litres (5 cups) water
1 large vegetable stock cube, crumbled
350g broccoli, chopped
2 medium carrots, chopped
4 medium zucchini, chopped
1 small red pepper, chopped

Melt butter in large saucepan, add leek, stir over medium heat for about 5 minutes (or microwave on HIGH for about 3 minutes) or until leek is soft. Stir in flour, stir over medium heat for 1 minute (or microwave on HIGH for 1 minute). Stir in water and stock cube, stir over high heat (or microwave on HIGH for about 3 minutes) until mixture boils and thickens.

Add vegetables, cover, simmer for about 10 minutes (or microwave on HIGH for about 10 minutes) or until vegetables are just tender.

Serves 4.

Back, from left: Kumara and Lentil Soup; Chunky Vegetable Soup. Front: Tomato and Pasta Soup.

Pots and boxes: Country Form; spoon: The Country Trader; tea-towel: Casa Shopping

Snacks

Making snack decisions will be a pleasure with our treats for different times and occasions. There are tasty light nibbles, child-pleasing snacks for school and after, picnic treats and dinner party appetisers. Some can be made ahead; others are best prepared just before serving.

TROPICAL MIX

Tropical mix can be made a week ahead; keep, covered, in refrigerator. This recipe is not suitable to freeze or microwave.

½ cup chopped dried apricots
½ cup chopped dates
½ cup sultanas
¼ cup flaked coconut
¼ cup slivered almonds
¼ cup rolled rice
2 tablespoons oil
1 tablespoon honey

Combine apricots, dates, sultanas, coconut, almonds and rice in large heatproof bowl. Combine oil and honey in small saucepan, bring to boil, boil for 1 minute. Pour honey mixture over fruit mixture; mix well. Spoon tropical mix into shallow baking dish, bake in moderate oven for 10 minutes, stirring occasionally; cool.
Makes about 2 cups.

ABOVE: Tropical Mix. RIGHT: Frozen Fruit Pops.

Jug: Barbara's House & Garden; bowl: Accoutrement (right)

FROZEN FRUIT POPS

Ice block moulds are available from large variety stores. You will need about 4 passionfruit for this recipe. Pops can be frozen for 2 weeks.

250g punnet strawberries, sliced
¼ cup passionfruit pulp
2 teaspoons grated orange rind
½ cup orange juice

Combine all ingredients in medium bowl. Spoon mixture into ice block moulds, cover with lids. Freeze pops for several hours or overnight.
Makes 12.

NUTTY AVOCADO SPREAD

Spread is best made just before serving. Recipe unsuitable to freeze.

1 small ripe avocado, chopped
1 tablespoon lemon juice
1 hard-boiled egg
¼ cup Brazil nuts, finely chopped
3 green shallots, finely chopped
1 tablespoon chopped fresh parsley
Blend or process avocado and juice until smooth. Push egg through sieve. Combine avocado mixture, egg, nuts, shallots and parsley in medium bowl, stir until well combined. Use mixture as a sandwich spread.

Makes about 1 cup.

BELOW: Carob Fruit Skewers. LEFT: From top: Nutty Avocado Spread; Pumpkin and Peanut Butter Lavash Rolls.

All accessories: Accoutrement (below); boxes: Country Form (left)

PUMPKIN AND PEANUT BUTTER LAVASH ROLLS

Rolls are best prepared as close to serving time as possible. Recipe unsuitable to freeze.

1 cup grated raw pumpkin
½ cup chopped celery
1 cup shredded lettuce
2 green shallots, chopped
4 pieces lavash bread
½ cup smooth peanut butter
Combine pumpkin, celery, lettuce and shallots in large bowl, mix well. Spread 1 side of bread evenly with peanut butter. Divide pumpkin mixture into 4 portions, sprinkle evenly over peanut butter. Roll bread up from narrow sides, slice before serving.

Serves 4.

CAROB FRUIT SKEWERS

Skewers can be made several hours ahead; keep, covered, in refrigerator. Recipe unsuitable to freeze.

100g milk carob, chopped
1 teaspoon oil
2 medium bananas
¾ cup crushed mixed nuts
250g punnet strawberries, halved
2 medium kiwi fruit, chopped
Place carob and oil into small heatproof bowl, place over small saucepan of simmering water (or microwave on HIGH for about 1 minute) until melted. Cut each banana into 8 slices, dip slices into carob mixture, toss in nuts, place onto trays, allow to set. Alternate pieces of coated banana, strawberries and kiwi fruit on wooden skewers.

Serves 4.

CREAMED SPINACH PATE

Pâté can be made a day ahead; keep, covered, in refrigerator. Recipe unsuitable to freeze or microwave.

2 bunches (80 leaves) English spinach
¼ cup water
1 large vegetable stock cube, crumbled
1 teaspoon ground nutmeg
1 teaspoon cornflour
1 teaspoon water, extra
30g butter
1 large onion, chopped
2 cloves garlic, crushed
¼ cup cream

Combine spinach, water, stock cube and nutmeg in large saucepan. Bring to boil, reduce heat, simmer, uncovered, for about 20 minutes, stirring occasionally, until liquid has evaporated and spinach is almost dry. Blend cornflour with extra water, add to pan, stir over medium heat until mixture boils; cool.

Melt butter in medium saucepan, add onion and garlic, stir over medium heat for about 3 minutes or until onion is soft, cool. Blend or process spinach mixture with onion mixture and cream until smooth. Transfer mixture to serving dish, cover; refrigerate for several hours or until firm.

TOMATO AND ONION PITA PIZZAS

This recipe is not suitable to freeze or microwave.

4 wholemeal pita pocket breads
½ cup bottled pasta sauce
1 cup grated tasty cheese
2 medium tomatoes, thinly sliced
1 medium onion, thinly sliced
¼ cup pitted black olives, halved

Place pocket breads in single layer on oven tray. Spread each pocket bread with pasta sauce, top with half the cheese, then the tomatoes, onion and olives, sprinkle with remaining cheese. Bake in hot oven for about 15 minutes or until lightly browned.

Makes 4.

HUMMUS ALFALFA POCKETS

Hummus can be made 2 days ahead; keep, covered, in refrigerator. Pockets are best filled just before serving. Recipe unsuitable to freeze.

2 x 425g cans garbanzos, drained
1 clove garlic, crushed
1 teaspoon grated lime rind
2 teaspoons lime juice
2 tablespoons chopped fresh
  oregano
¼ teaspoon tabasco sauce
1 teaspoon grated fresh ginger
2 tablespoons water, approximately
8 wholemeal pita pocket breads
6 medium tomatoes, chopped
alfalfa sprouts

Blend or process garbanzos, garlic, rind, juice, oregano, sauce and ginger until smooth. Add enough water to hummus mixture to make a paste consistency. Divide hummus between pocket breads, top with tomatoes and alfalfa sprouts.

Makes 8.

SWEET CORN WAFFLES WITH CHUTNEY AND SALAD

Waffles can be frozen for 2 months. Salad unsuitable to freeze. Recipe unsuitable to microwave.

1 cup wholemeal plain flour
¾ cup white plain flour
¼ cup white self-raising flour
1 teaspoon ground cumin
1 tablespoon castor sugar
2 eggs, separated
1¾ cups milk
60g butter, melted
2 tablespoons water
310g can creamed corn
½ cup chutney
SALAD
1 butter lettuce
1 medium carrot, sliced
1 small avocado, sliced
½ x 250g punnet cherry tomatoes,
  halved
1 small green cucumber, sliced
¼ cup olive oil
¼ cup cider vinegar
1 teaspoon curry powder

Sift flours, cumin and sugar into large bowl, make well in centre, gradually stir in combined egg yolks and milk, then butter, water and corn. Fold in softly beaten egg whites. Drop about 2 tablespoons of mixture onto waffle iron. Close iron, cook for about 2 minutes or until golden brown. Serve waffles with chutney and salad.

Salad: Combine roughly torn lettuce leaves, carrot, avocado, tomatoes and cucumber in large bowl. Combine oil, vinegar and curry powder in jar, shake well. Pour over salad just before serving, toss gently.

Serves 6.

RYE SAVOURY PIKELETS

Pikelet batter can be prepared 2 hours ahead; keep, covered, in refrigerator. Cook just before serving. Recipe unsuitable to freeze or microwave.

½ cup rye flour
½ cup white self-raising flour
¼ teaspoon ground nutmeg
1 teaspoon sugar
1 egg, lightly beaten
1 cup milk, approximately
1 teaspoon cider vinegar
15g butter, melted
½ cup grated tasty cheese
¼ cup grated parmesan cheese
2 tablespoons chopped fresh parsley
2 tablespoons sunflower seed
  kernels

Sift flours, nutmeg and sugar into medium bowl, make well in centre. Gradually stir in combined egg, milk and vinegar, stir until smooth (or blend or process all ingredients until smooth). Stir in butter, cheeses, parsley and kernels. Drop dessertspoons of batter into heated greased heavy-based frying pan, cook over medium heat until bubbles start to appear, turn pikelets, cook until golden brown on other side.

Makes about 20.

BELOW: Hummus Alfalfa Pockets. BELOW LEFT: Tomato and Onion Pita Pizzas ABOVE LEFT: Creamed Spinach Pate.

All accessories: Accoutrement (below); pâté pots: Accoutrement; tea-towel: Barbara's House & Garden (above left)

WHOLEMEAL TARTLETS WITH MUSHROOM FILLING

Filling can be made a day ahead; keep, covered, in refrigerator. Recipe unsuitable to freeze.

PASTRY
½ cup wholemeal plain flour
½ cup white plain flour
45g butter
1 teaspoon grated lemon rind
1 egg yolk, lightly beaten
2 tablespoons lemon juice, approximately
⅓ cup grated tasty cheese
MUSHROOM FILLING
30g butter
5 green shallots, chopped
375g mushrooms, chopped
1 tablespoon white plain flour
¼ cup skim milk
¼ cup grated parmesan cheese

Pastry: Lightly grease 12 shallow patty pans. Sift flours into medium bowl, rub in butter. Stir in rind, egg yolk and enough juice to mix to a firm dough. Turn pastry onto lightly floured surface, knead lightly until smooth, cover, refrigerate for 30 minutes. Roll pastry out thinly, cut out 12 x 8cm rounds, press into prepared pans, trim edges.

Cover each case with greaseproof paper, fill with dried beans or rice, bake in moderately hot oven for 5 minutes. Remove beans and paper, bake further 5 minutes or until golden brown, cool. Place 1 level tablespoon of filling into each case, sprinkle with tasty cheese. Bake in moderately hot oven for about 10 minutes or until cheese has melted.

Mushroom Filling: Melt butter in medium saucepan, add shallots and mushrooms, stir over low heat for about 5 minutes (or microwave on HIGH for about 4 minutes) or until liquid has evaporated. Stir in flour, stir over medium heat for 1 minute (or microwave on HIGH for 1 minute). Remove from heat, gradually stir in milk, stir over high heat (or microwave on HIGH for about 2 minutes) until mixture boils and thickens; cool. Stir in parmesan cheese.

Makes 12.

OLIVE CHEESE BITES

Cheese bites can be made several hours ahead; keep in airtight container. This recipe is not suitable to freeze or microwave.

½ cup white plain flour
½ cup wholemeal plain flour
¼ teaspoon chilli powder
90g butter, chopped
2 tablespoons grated tasty cheese
2 tablespoons grated parmesan cheese
2 teaspoons chopped fresh chives
1 egg, lightly beaten
24 large stuffed green olives

Sift flours and chilli powder into medium bowl, rub in butter. Stir in cheeses and chives, stir in enough of the egg to make a stiff dough. Press dough into a ball, cover, refrigerate for 30 minutes. Roll dough out thinly on well-floured surface, cut into 24 rounds with an 8cm cutter.

Rinse olives under cold water, drain on absorbent paper. Wrap each olive in a pastry round, place on oven tray. Bake in moderately hot oven for about 25 minutes or until golden brown; cool on tray. Serve warm or cold.

Makes 24.

CHEESY MILLET MUFFINS

Muffins can be frozen for 2 months. Use microwave-proof muffin pan for microwave oven.

1 cup wholemeal self-raising flour
1 cup millet meal
½ cup grated fresh parmesan cheese
2 tablespoons chopped fresh parsley
½ cup soy milk
1 egg, lightly beaten
90g butter, melted
2 tablespoons hulled millet

Lightly grease 12 patty pans. Sift flour into large bowl, stir in millet meal, cheese and parsley. Make well in centre, use a fork to stir in combined soy milk, egg and butter.

Spoon mixture into prepared pans, sprinkle with hulled millet. Bake in moderately hot oven for about 20 minutes or until lightly browned (or microwave half the muffins on HIGH for about 3 minutes, then repeat with remaining mixture). Serve muffins with butter, if desired.

Makes about 12.

Clockwise from top left: Sweet Corn Waffles with Chutney and Salad; Wholemeal Tartlets with Mushroom Filling; Olive Cheese Bites; Rye Savoury Pikelets; Cheesy Millet Muffins.

ALFALFA BALLS WITH TAHINI SAUCE

Recipe can be made several hours ahead; keep, covered, in refrigerator. This recipe is not suitable to freeze or microwave.

6 slices wholemeal bread, chopped
2 medium onions, chopped
1 cup walnut pieces
2 tablespoons arrowroot
1 teaspoon ground cumin
¼ teaspoon ground coriander
½ large vegetable stock cube, crumbled
1 cup alfalfa sprouts
2 teaspoons water, approximately
oil for shallow-frying

BROAD BEAN AND TOFU DIP

Dip can be made a day ahead; keep, covered, in refrigerator. Recipe unsuitable to freeze.

500g fresh or frozen broad beans
250g soft tofu, chopped
2 tablespoons orange juice
1 tablespoon chopped fresh basil

Boil, steam or microwave broad beans until soft; cool. Remove skin from beans, discard skins. Blend or process all ingredients until smooth, spoon into serving dish; refrigerate for 1 hour before serving. Serve with fresh crunchy vegetables.

Makes about 2 cups.

ABOVE: Broad Bean and Tofu Dip.
RIGHT: From left: Alfalfa Balls with Tahini Sauce; Curried Corn Fritters with Minted Sour Cream.

Plate: Shop 3, Balmain; dishes: Villa Italiana; rug: Mosmania (right)

TAHINI SAUCE

½ cup plain yoghurt
1 tablespoon tahini
½ small green cucumber, chopped
1 teaspoon light soy sauce
1 tablespoon water

Blend or process bread, onions, walnuts, arrowroot, cumin, coriander and stock cube until smooth. Combine mixture with alfalfa sprouts in medium bowl, stir in enough water to bind mixture together (if necessary). Roll mixture into 2cm balls, shallow-fry in hot oil for about 2 minutes or until golden brown, drain on absorbent paper. Serve hot with tahini sauce.
Tahini Sauce: Combine all ingredients in small bowl, mix well.

CURRIED CORN FRITTERS WITH MINTED SOUR CREAM

Batter can be prepared several hours ahead; keep, covered, in refrigerator. Fritters are best cooked just before serving. Minted sour cream can be prepared up to a day ahead; keep, covered, in refrigerator. Recipe unsuitable to freeze or microwave.

1 cup wholemeal plain flour
2 teaspoons curry powder
2 eggs, lightly beaten
¾ cup milk
1 medium onion, grated
310g can corn kernels, drained
oil for shallow-frying

MINTED SOUR CREAM

1 cup sour light cream
1 tablespoon chopped fresh mint

Sift flour and curry powder into large bowl, make well in centre, gradually stir in combined eggs and milk, mix to a smooth batter (or blend or process all ingredients until smooth). Cover, stand for 30 minutes. Stir in onion and corn. Shallow-fry tablespoons of batter in hot oil in medium frying pan for about 2 minutes each side or until golden brown. Drain on absorbent paper. Serve with minted sour cream.
Minted Sour Cream: Combine sour cream and mint in small bowl, mix well.
   Makes about 20.

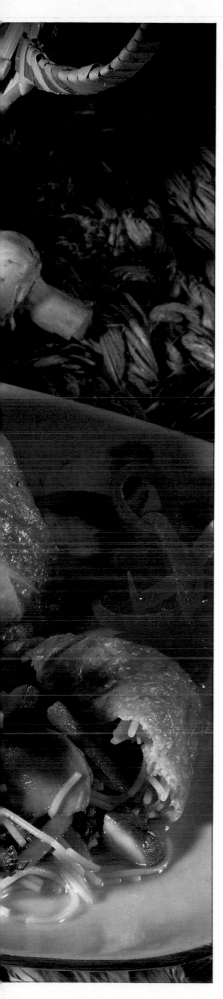

Lunches

We have plenty of fresh ideas about lunches, ranging from pastries to paella, croquettes and crépes and more. Variety is the key to enjoyment, whether you want a light meal or a hearty one. Some recipes can also be served as dinner party entrées.

VEGETABLE TOFU POCKETS

Pockets can be prepared a day ahead; keep, covered, in refrigerator. Recipe unsuitable to freeze or microwave.

1 strip dried gourd
8 deep-fried tofu squares
3 cups water
3 teaspoons dashi concentrate
2 tablespoons teriyaki sauce
1 tablespoon dry sherry
TASTY VEGETABLE FILLING
60g vermicelli noodles
3 medium spinach (silverbeet)
 leaves, chopped
100g oyster mushrooms, chopped
2 small carrots, finely chopped
2 small zucchini, finely chopped
¼ cup water
¼ teaspoon dashi concentrate
1 tablespoon teriyaki sauce
1 teaspoon dry sherry
½ teaspoon sugar

Cut gourd into 8cm x 10cm lengths. Place tofu squares and gourd strips into medium bowl, cover with boiling water; stand for 15 minutes. Squeeze excess water from tofu, cut a thin strip from 1 edge of each square, pull cut edges apart to make pockets. Divide filling evenly between pockets, tie open edges with drained gourd strips.

Combine water, dashi, sauce and sherry in large saucepan, bring to boil, add tofu pockets; reduce heat, cover, simmer for 15 minutes, lift carefully from liquid.

Tasty Vegetable Filling: Add noodles gradually to large saucepan of boiling water, boil, uncovered, for 3 minutes, drain. Combine noodles with remaining ingredients in large saucepan, bring to boil, reduce heat, cover, simmer for about 5 minutes or until vegetables are just tender.

Makes 8.

LETTUCE PARCELS WITH CARROT SAUCE

Parcels are best prepared close to serving time. Carrot sauce can be made a day ahead; keep, covered, in refrigerator. This recipe is not suitable to freeze.

5 medium potatoes
1 medium carrot, grated
2½ cups shredded cabbage
30g butter
2 medium onions, chopped
2 cloves garlic, crushed
¾ cup grated tasty cheese
1 tablespoon sunflower seed
 kernels, chopped
1 tablespoon linseeds
2 tablespoons chopped fresh parsley
2 tablespoons chopped fresh
 coriander
8 iceberg lettuce leaves
CARROT SAUCE
3 medium carrots
2 cups water
1 large vegetable stock cube,
 crumbled

Boil, steam or microwave potatoes until tender; drain. Mash potatoes in large bowl. Boil, steam or microwave carrot and cabbage until tender; drain, add to potato; mix well.

Melt butter in small frying pan, add onions and garlic, stir over medium heat for about 3 minutes (or microwave on HIGH for about 4 minutes) or until onions are soft. Add to potato mixture with cheese, kernels, linseeds and herbs; mix well.

Drop lettuce leaves into large saucepan of boiling water, drain immediately; rinse under cold water, drain on absorbent paper. Divide potato mixture evenly over lettuce leaves, roll up firmly. Serve with sauce.

Carrot Sauce: Combine carrots, water and stock cube in medium saucepan, bring to boil, reduce heat, cover, simmer for about 20 minutes (or microwave on HIGH for about 6 minutes) or until carrots are tender. Blend or process until smooth, reheat if necessary.

Serves 4.

Vegetable Tofu Pockets.

Plate: Antique General Store

CHILLI LENTIL LOAF

Loaf can be made a day ahead; keep, covered, in refrigerator. Recipe unsuitable to freeze or microwave.

1 cup brown lentils
1 medium carrot, finely grated
1 stick celery, chopped
2 small fresh red chillies, finely chopped
1 cup stale wholemeal breadcrumbs
1 tablespoon tomato paste
1 medium onion, finely chopped
1 egg, lightly beaten

Lightly grease 14cm x 21cm loaf pan, line base with paper, grease paper. Add lentils to large saucepan of boiling water, boil, covered, for about 1 hour or until tender, drain; cool. Blend or process half the lentils until smooth. Combine all lentils, carrot, celery, chillies, breadcrumbs, paste, onion and egg in large bowl; mix well. Press mixture into prepared pan, bake in moderate oven for about 1 hour or until firm to touch. Stand for 5 minutes before turning out.

Serves 4.

CARROT ZUCCHINI CROQUETTES

Croquettes can be prepared a day ahead. This recipe is not suitable to freeze or microwave.

2 large carrots, grated
1 large zucchini, grated
4 green shallots, chopped
1 tablespoon chopped fresh coriander
⅓ cup packaged ground hazelnuts
2 tablespoons wholemeal plain flour
30g butter, melted
⅓ cup wholemeal plain flour, extra
2 eggs, lightly beaten
2 tablespoons water
1 cup stale wholemeal breadcrumbs
⅓ cup sesame seeds
oil for shallow-frying

Combine carrots, zucchini, shallots, coriander, hazelnuts, flour and butter in large bowl, mix well. Divide mixture into 10 equal portions, shape portions into croquettes. Toss croquettes in extra flour, shake away excess flour, dip in combined eggs and water, then combined breadcrumbs and sesame seeds. Dip croquettes into egg mixture again, then in breadcrumb mixture. Place croquettes onto tray, refrigerate for 1 hour. Shallow-fry in hot oil until golden brown all over.

Makes 10.

RIGHT: Clockwise from left: Crêpe-Wrapped Corn and Bean Loaf; Carrot Zucchini Croquettes; Chilli Lentil Loaf. ABOVE: Lettuce Parcels with Carrot Sauce.

Plate: Shop 3, Balmain; plant: Sherringham's Nursery (above); plates: Villa Italiana; background shutter and cutlery; Appley Hoare Antiques (right)

CREPE-WRAPPED CORN AND BEAN LOAF

Unfilled crêpes can be made up to 2 days ahead; keep, layered with greaseproof paper, in refrigerator. Crêpes can be frozen for 2 months. Corn and bean mixtures can be prepared a day ahead. Recipe unsuitable to freeze or microwave.

CREPES
⅓ cup white plain flour
1½ tablespoons polenta
1 egg, lightly beaten
⅔ cup milk
1 teaspoon olive oil
CHILLI BEAN LAYER
310g can red kidney beans, drained
1 tablespoon tomato paste
1 small fresh red chilli, finely chopped
1 egg, separated
2 teaspoons chopped fresh oregano
CORN LAYER
310g can corn kernels, drained
1 teaspoon curry powder
1 egg, separated
1 tablespoon chopped fresh chives

Crêpes: Line 8cm x 26cm bar pan with foil, grease foil. Sift flour into bowl, stir in polenta, make well in centre, gradually stir in combined egg, milk and oil, mix to a smooth batter (or blend or process all ingredients until smooth). Cover, stand for 30 minutes. Pour 2 to 3 tablespoons of batter into heated greased small heavy-based crêpe pan; cook until lightly browned underneath. Turn crêpe, brown on other side. Repeat with remaining batter. You will need 6 crêpes for this recipe.

Line prepared pan with 2 crêpes, trim crêpes to fit. Spoon in bean layer, cover with 2 trimmed crêpes. Spoon in corn layer, top with 2 crêpes. Trim edges, cover loaf with greased foil, bake in moderate oven for about 50 minutes or until loaf is firm. Stand for 5 minutes before turning onto wire rack. Carefully remove foil before serving warm or cold.

Chilli Bean Layer: Blend or process beans, paste, chilli and egg yolk until smooth, transfer mixture to medium bowl, fold in softly beaten egg white and oregano.

Corn Layer: Blend or process corn, curry powder and egg yolk until smooth, transfer mixture to medium bowl, fold in softly beaten egg white and chives.

Serves 4.

From left: Mushroom Spinach Strudel; Crumbed Parsnip Sticks with Mustard Yoghurt.

Wooden box: Antique General Store

CRUMBED PARSNIP STICKS WITH MUSTARD YOGHURT

Parsnip sticks and dressing can be prepared a day ahead; keep, covered, in refrigerator. Deep-fry sticks just before serving. Recipe unsuitable to freeze or microwave.

3 medium parsnips
2 eggs, lightly beaten
¼ cup milk
2 tablespoons wholemeal plain flour
2 cups (200g) stale wholemeal breadcrumbs
oil for deep-frying

MUSTARD YOGHURT
1 cup plain yoghurt
2 tablespoons seeded mustard

Cut parsnips into thin sticks, dip into combined eggs and milk, toss in flour. Dip sticks into egg mixture again, drain off excess, then toss in breadcrumbs, pressing breadcrumbs on firmly. Deep-fry sticks in hot oil in batches until golden brown and tender; drain on absorbent paper. Serve hot sticks with mustard yoghurt.

Mustard Yoghurt: Combine yoghurt and mustard in a small bowl; mix well.

Serves 4.

MUSHROOM SPINACH STRUDEL

Strudel is best prepared just before serving. This recipe is not suitable to freeze or microwave.

8 medium spinach (silverbeet) leaves
2 tablespoons oil
300g mushrooms, sliced
6 green shallots, chopped
½ cup cottage cheese
¼ teaspoon ground nutmeg
1 egg, lightly beaten
6 sheets fillo pastry
45g butter, melted
2 teaspoons packaged breadcrumbs

Boil, steam or microwave spinach until soft, squeeze out as much excess liquid as possible. Chop spinach finely, place in medium bowl.

Heat oil in medium frying pan, add mushrooms and shallots, stir over medium heat until mushrooms are soft; drain. Add to spinach with cheese, nutmeg and egg, stir well; cool to room temperature.

Brush 1 sheet of pastry lightly with butter, top with another sheet of pastry, brush with butter. Repeat with remaining pastry and most of the butter. Spoon mushroom mixture along long edge of pastry, fold sides in, roll up like a Swiss roll, place on oven tray. Brush roll all over with remaining butter, sprinkle with breadcrumbs. Bake in moderately hot oven for about 25 minutes or until lightly browned.

Serves 6.

BEANS AND PEPPERS WITH POLENTA TRIANGLES

Polenta can be prepared up to 2 days ahead; keep, covered, in refrigerator. Recipe is best made just before serving. This recipe is not suitable to freeze or microwave.

1 litre (4 cups) water
2 large vegetable stock cubes, crumbled
1 cup polenta
oil for shallow-frying
250g green beans
30g butter
2 medium red peppers, sliced
1 medium green pepper, sliced
¼ cup olive oil
2 tablespoons cider vinegar
1 clove garlic, crushed
2 teaspoons chopped fresh basil

Lightly oil 19cm x 29cm lamington pan. Combine water and stock cubes in large saucepan, bring to boil. Gradually add polenta to water, stirring constantly. Reduce heat, cover, simmer for 30 minutes, stirring frequently. Spread polenta evenly into prepared pan, cool; stand for 2 hours. Cut polenta into 12 squares, cut each square in half diagonally.

Shallow-fry polenta in hot oil for about 5 minutes each side or until golden brown.

Boil, steam or microwave beans until just tender, rinse under cold water. Melt butter in large frying pan, add peppers, stir over medium heat for 3 minutes. Combine oil, vinegar, garlic and basil with beans, add to peppers, stir over medium heat further 2 minutes. Serve with hot polenta.

Serves 6.

ABOVE: From top: Beans and Peppers with Polenta Triangles; Cheese Pasties with Tomato Basil Sauce. RIGHT: Eggplant Chips with Pimiento Sauce.

Plate and jug: Corso de Fiori (right); black dish: Australian East India Co; board and jug: Oldentime Antiquew; green serving ware: Made where (above)

EGGPLANT CHIPS WITH PIMIENTO SAUCE

Cook eggplant close to serving time. Sauce can be made up to 2 days ahead; keep, covered, in refrigerator. This recipe is not suitable to freeze or microwave.

2 medium eggplants
salt
cornflour
oil for deep-frying
BATTER
1 cup white self-raising flour
½ teaspoon chilli powder
¾ cup water
2 eggs, lightly beaten
PIMIENTO SAUCE
1 tablespoon olive oil
1 medium onion, thinly sliced
1 clove garlic, crushed
1 teaspoon cornflour
¾ cup water
½ cup tomato purée
200g can pimientos, drained, sliced

CHEESE PASTIES WITH TOMATO BASIL SAUCE

Pasties can be prepared a day ahead; keep, covered, in refrigerator. Recipe unsuitable to freeze. Sauce suitable to microwave.

1½ cups wholemeal plain flour
½ cup white plain flour
½ cup white self-raising flour
185g butter
2 teaspoons lemon juice
¼ cup water, approximately
RICOTTA CHEESE FILLING
¾ cup ricotta cheese
¼ cup grated parmesan cheese
1 egg, lightly beaten
1 medium tomato, chopped
60g baby mushrooms, sliced
1 teaspoon chopped fresh basil
2 tablespoons chopped fresh parsley
BASIL SAUCE
15g butter
1 medium onion, chopped
1 clove garlic, crushed
425g can tomatoes
200g baby mushrooms, sliced
2 teaspoons raw sugar
1 tablespoon chopped fresh basil

Sift flours into medium bowl, rub in butter, add juice and enough water to make a stiff dough. Turn dough onto lightly floured surface, knead until smooth, cover, refrigerate 30 minutes.

Roll dough out on lightly floured surface to 35cm x 45cm rectangle, cut into 12 rounds with 10cm cutter.

Place level tablespoons of filling onto centre of each round, lightly brush edges with water, press edges together to seal, place onto oven tray, prick top of pasties with fork. Bake in hot oven for about 25 minutes or until lightly browned. Serve with sauce.

Ricotta Cheese Filling: Combine all ingredients in medium bowl; mix well.

Basil Sauce: Melt butter in small saucepan, add onion and garlic, stir over medium heat for about 2 minutes (or microwave on HIGH for about 3 minutes) or until onion is soft. Blend or process un-drained tomatoes, add to onion mixture, stir in mushrooms, sugar and basil. Bring to boil, reduce heat, simmer, uncovered, for about 5 minutes (or microwave on HIGH for about 5 minutes) or until sauce thickens slightly.

Makes 12.

Cut eggplants into strips, place onto wire rack, sprinkle with salt, stand for 30 minutes. Rinse eggplants under cold water, drain, pat dry with absorbent paper. Toss eggplants in cornflour, shake off excess cornflour, dip into batter. Deep-fry eggplant chips a few at a time in hot oil until golden brown, drain on absorbent paper. Serve hot with sauce.

Batter: Sift flour and chilli powder into large bowl, make well in centre, gradually stir in water and eggs, mix to a smooth batter (or blend or process all ingredients until smooth).

Pimiento Sauce: Heat oil in medium saucepan, add onion and garlic, stir over medium heat for about 2 minutes (or microwave on HIGH for about 3 minutes) or until onion is soft. Blend cornflour with 2 tablespoons of the water, add to saucepan with remaining water, purée and pimientos, stir over high heat (or microwave on HIGH) until sauce boils and thickens slightly.

Serves 4.

EGGPLANT SPREAD WITH LEBANESE BREAD

Spread can be made 2 days ahead; keep, covered, in refrigerator. Bread can be frozen for up to 2 months.

1 large eggplant, peeled, chopped
salt
2 tablespoons oil
1 clove garlic, crushed
¼ cup tahini
2 tablespoons lemon juice
¼ teaspoon paprika
LEBANESE BREAD
15g compressed yeast
½ teaspoon sugar
1¼ cups warm water
2½ cups white plain flour
1 tablespoon oil

Place eggplant on wire rack, sprinkle with salt; stand for 20 minutes. Rinse eggplant under cold water, drain on absorbent paper.

Heat oil in medium saucepan, add eggplant and garlic, stir over low heat for about 10 minutes (or microwave on HIGH for about 6 minutes) or until tender. Blend or process eggplant mixture, tahini and juice until smooth. Transfer mixture to dish, sprinkle with paprika. Serve with crisp fresh vegetables and warm Lebanese bread.

Lebanese Bread: Combine yeast, sugar and water in small bowl, stir until sugar is dissolved. Stand in warm place for about 10 minutes or until mixture is foamy.

Sift flour into large bowl, make well in centre, stir in yeast mixture and oil, mix to a soft dough. Turn dough onto floured surface, knead for about 3 minutes or until smooth and elastic. Return dough to large oiled bowl, cover, stand in warm place for about 20 minutes or until dough has doubled in bulk.

Turn dough onto lightly floured surface, knead until smooth. Divide dough into 4, cover 3 pieces, roll remaining piece into 25cm circle. Place circle onto lightly oiled oven tray, bake in hot oven for about 4 minutes or until puffed and lightly browned. Wrap in clean cloth, stand for 3 minutes. Repeat with remaining dough.

Serves 4.

STIR-FRIED VEGETABLES WITH LEMON GINGER SAUCE

Prepare recipe just before serving. Recipe unsuitable to freeze.

½ cup blanched almonds
2 tablespoons oil
1 medium onion, chopped
2 cloves garlic, crushed
1 medium green pepper, chopped
250g green beans, chopped
¼ medium cauliflower, chopped
¼ small cabbage, shredded
2 medium zucchini, chopped
1 tablespoon cornflour
¾ cup water
1 cup bean sprouts
¼ cup tamari shoyu
2 teaspoons lemon juice
1 tablespoon grated fresh ginger
¼ teaspoon ground cardamom
1 tablespoon sugar

Toast almonds on oven tray in moderate oven for about 5 minutes, cool. Heat oil in large frying pan or wok, add onion and garlic, stir over medium heat for about 2 minutes (or microwave on HIGH for about 3 minutes) or until onion is soft. Add pepper, beans and cauliflower, stir over medium heat for about 5 minutes (or microwave on HIGH for about 3 minutes) or until cauliflower is almost tender. Add cabbage and zucchini, stir over heat for about 2 minutes (or microwave on HIGH for about 1 minute) or until cabbage is wilted.

Blend cornflour with water, add to pan with sprouts, tamari shoyu, juice, ginger, cardamom and sugar, stir over high heat (or microwave on HIGH for about 3 minutes) until mixture boils and thickens. Sprinkle with almonds just before serving.

Serves 4.

PASTA WITH TOMATOES AND CASHEW NUT BALLS

We used spiral pasta in this recipe. Sauce and cashew nut balls can be made up to 2 days ahead; keep, covered in refrigerator. This recipe is unsuitable to freeze.

3 cups (250g) wholemeal pasta
TOMATO SAUCE
30g butter
1 clove garlic, crushed
1 large onion, chopped
4 large tomatoes, chopped
2 tablespoons tomato paste
2 teaspoons chopped fresh oregano
1½ cups water
CASHEW NUT BALLS
2 cups (300g) unsalted, unroasted cashew nuts
2 eggs, lightly beaten
1 cup stale wholemeal breadcrumbs
1½ tablespoons oil

Add pasta gradually to large saucepan of boiling water, boil, uncovered, for about 12 minutes or until tender, drain. Serve pasta with tomato sauce and cashew nut balls.

Tomato Sauce: Melt butter in medium saucepan, add garlic and onion, stir over medium heat for about 2 minutes (or microwave on HIGH for about 3 minutes) or until onion is soft. Add tomatoes, paste, oregano and water, bring to boil, reduce heat, simmer, uncovered, for about 20 minutes (or microwave on HIGH for about 25 minutes) or until sauce is slightly thickened. Add cashew nut balls to sauce, reheat before serving.

Cashew Nut Balls: Blend or process nuts finely. Combine nuts, eggs and breadcrumbs in large bowl, mix well. Shape mixture into 3cm balls. Heat oil in medium frying pan, add cashew nut balls, cook over medium heat for about 3 minutes or until golden brown, drain on absorbent paper.

Serves 4.

VEGETARIAN PAELLA

Paella is best made just before serving. This recipe is not suitable to freeze or microwave.

1 tablespoon olive oil
1 clove garlic, crushed
1 medium onion, sliced
1 cup long grain rice
500g broccoli, chopped
¼ medium cauliflower, chopped
410g can tomatoes
2 cups water
1 large carrot, finely chopped
1 medium red pepper, chopped
1 medium green pepper, chopped
1 teaspoon paprika
2 teaspoons chopped fresh oregano

Heat oil in large saucepan, add garlic and onion, stir over medium heat for about 2 minutes or until onion is soft. Add rice, stir over medium heat for 3 minutes. Stir in broccoli, cauliflower, undrained crushed tomatoes and water. Bring to boil, boil, uncovered, for about 10 minutes or until rice is tender and most of the liquid is absorbed. Add remaining ingredients, mix well. Reduce heat, cover, simmer for about 5 minutes or until peppers are soft.

Serves 4.

Clockwise from top: Eggplant Spread with Lebanese Bread; Stir-Fried Vegetables with Lemon Ginger Sauce; Pasta with Tomatoes and Cashew Nut Balls; Vegetarian Paella.

Plates: Corso de Fiori; table, tray and basket: The Country Trader

NUTTY MILLET AND RICE PILAF

Prepare pilaf just before serving. This recipe is not suitable to freeze or microwave.

15g butter
1 medium onion, chopped
1 cup long grain rice
¾ cup hulled millet
1½ cups water
½ large vegetable stock cube, crumbled
1 cup cooked green peas
¾ cup walnut pieces

Melt butter in medium saucepan, add onion, stir over medium heat for about 2 minutes or until onion is soft. Add rice and millet, stir to coat grains with butter. Add water and stock cube, bring to boil, reduce heat, cover tightly, cook over very low heat for 12 minutes. Remove from heat, add peas, cover tightly, stand further 15 minutes, stir gently with fork. Add nuts.

Serves 4.

SPAGHETTI SQUASH WITH BROCCOLI SAUCE

Recipe is best made close to serving time. Recipe unsuitable to freeze.

2kg spaghetti squash
BROCCOLI SAUCE
500g broccoli, chopped
1 medium carrot, chopped
30g butter
1 medium onion, chopped
1 tablespoon white plain flour
¾ cup milk
¼ cup plain yoghurt
1 teaspoon French mustard

Cut squash into large pieces crossways. Steam or microwave squash until just tender, fork flesh away from skin to make spaghetti-like threads; drain. Serve with sauce.

Broccoli Sauce: Boil, steam or microwave broccoli and carrot until tender, drain.

Melt butter in medium saucepan, add onion, stir over medium heat for about 2 minutes (or microwave on HIGH for about 3 minutes) or until onion is soft. Stir in flour, stir over medium heat for 1 minute (or microwave on HIGH for 1 minute).

Remove from heat, gradually stir in combined milk, yoghurt and mustard, stir over high heat (or microwave on HIGH for about 3 minutes) until mixture boils and thickens. Add broccoli and carrot, stir over low heat (or microwave on HIGH for 2 minutes) until hot.

Serves 4.

Clockwise from top left: Vegetable Nut Crumble; Nutty Millet and Rice Pilaf; Spaghetti Squash with Broccoli Sauce; Tofu and Sesame Tartlets; Kumara Croquettes with Sweet Dipping Sauce.

Plates: Accoutrement; table: The Country Trader

KUMARA CROQUETTES WITH SWEET DIPPING SAUCE

Croquettes can be made 12 hours before serving. Sauce can be made a day ahead; keep, covered, in the refrigerator. Sauce is not suitable to microwave.

2 medium kumaras, chopped
45g butter
4 green shallots, chopped
⅓ cup white plain flour
¾ cup milk
¾ cup grated tasty cheese
⅔ cup stale wholemeal breadcrumbs
2 eggs, lightly beaten
½ cup milk, extra
2 cups packaged breadcrumbs
oil for deep-frying
SWEET DIPPING SAUCE
1 cup white vinegar
1 cup castor sugar
1 small carrot, grated
1 small green cucumber, chopped
1 tablespoon chopped fresh chives
1 small fresh red chilli, finely
   chopped
pinch paprika

Boil, steam or microwave kumaras until tender, drain well. Mash in large bowl until smooth, cool. Melt butter in small saucepan, add shallots, stir over medium heat for 1 minute (or microwave on HIGH for 1 minute).

Stir in flour, stir over medium heat for 1 minute (or microwave on HIGH for 1 minute). Remove from heat, gradually stir in milk, stir over high heat (or microwave on HIGH for 3 minutes) until mixture boils and thickens, cool. Add shallot mixture to kumaras, stir in cheese and stale breadcrumbs.

Spread mixture onto tray covered with plastic wrap, cover, refrigerate until cold. Shape mixture into 16 croquettes. Dip croquettes into combined eggs and extra milk, then toss in packaged breadcrumbs. Deep-fry croquettes in hot oil a few at a time until golden brown, drain on absorbent paper. Serve with sauce

Sweet Dipping Sauce: Combine vinegar and sugar in small saucepan, stir over heat, without boiling, until sugar has dissolved. Bring to boil, boil, uncovered, without stirring, for about 3 minutes or until thickened slightly, cool for 5 minutes. Pour over combined carrot, cucumber, chives and chilli in a small bowl, cool. Sprinkle with paprika before serving.

Makes 16.

VEGETABLE NUT CRUMBLE

Crumble can be made a day ahead; keep, covered, in refrigerator. Recipe unsuitable to freeze.

1 cup brown rice
½ large vegetable stock cube,
   crumbled
1 egg
30g butter
1 small onion, chopped
1 small red pepper, chopped
125g broccoli, chopped
125g cauliflower, chopped
100g baby mushrooms, sliced
425g can tomatoes
1 tablespoon chopped fresh parsley
½ teaspoon dried mixed herbs
1 cup grated tasty cheese
NUTTY CRUMB TOPPING
15g butter, melted
¾ cup stale wholemeal breadcrumbs
1 cup chopped unsalted mixed nuts
2 teaspoons chopped fresh parsley

Add rice and stock cube to large saucepan of boiling water, boil rapidly, uncovered, for about 30 minutes or until tender; drain. Combine rice and egg in medium bowl; mix well. Spread mixture evenly over base of greased ovenproof dish (2 litre capacity).

Melt butter in large frying pan, add onion, stir over medium heat for about 2 minutes (or microwave on HIGH for about 3 minutes) or until onion is soft. Add pepper, broccoli, cauliflower, mushrooms, undrained crushed tomatoes, parsley and herbs, bring to boil. Reduce heat, cover, simmer for about 7 minutes (or microwave on HIGH for about 7 minutes) or until vegetables are tender. Spoon vegetables evenly over rice.

Sprinkle evenly with cheese, then topping. Bake in moderate oven for about 20 minutes (or microwave on HIGH for about 7 minutes).

Nutty Crumb Topping: Combine all ingredients in a small bowl, mix well.

TOFU AND SESAME TARTLETS

Unfilled tartlet cases can be made up to 2 days ahead; keep in airtight container, or freeze for up to 2 months. Fill cases just before serving.

PASTRY
⅔ cup wholemeal plain flour
⅓ cup white plain flour
60g butter
¼ cup sesame seeds
1 egg yolk
1 tablespoon water, approximately
FILLING
300g packet firm tofu
30g butter
2 medium onions, sliced
2 sticks celery, chopped
1 small red pepper, chopped
1 teaspoon cornflour
⅓ cup water
2 teaspoons seeded mustard
¼ large vegetable stock cube,
   crumbled
1 tablespoon chopped fresh parsley

RIGHT: Asparagus Timbales. ABOVE RIGHT: From top: Marinated Bean Sprout and Sesame Salad; Herbed Tomatoes with Cracked Wheat.

Chair: Mid-City Home & Garden (above right)

Pastry: Grease 4 x 9cm flan tins. Sift flours into medium bowl, rub in butter, stir in sesame seeds. Add egg yolk and enough water to mix to a firm dough. Turn pastry onto lightly floured surface, knead lightly until smooth. Cover, refrigerate for 30 minutes. Divide pastry into 4 portions. Roll portions large enough to line prepared tins.

Cover each pastry case with greaseproof paper, fill with dried beans or rice. Bake in moderately hot oven for 7 minutes, remove beans and paper, bake further 7 minutes or until lightly browned, cool. Remove pastry cases from tins, fill with tofu and vegetable filling.

Filling: Place tofu in medium bowl, cover with water, stand for 15 minutes, drain. Cut into 2cm cubes. Melt butter in medium saucepan, add onions, stir over medium heat for about 3 minutes (or microwave on HIGH for about 4 minutes) or until onions are soft. Add celery and pepper, stir over medium heat for 1 minute (or microwave on HIGH for 1 minute).

Blend cornflour with water, add mustard and stock cube, stir into onion mixture, stir over high heat (or microwave on HIGH for about 1 minute) until mixture boils and thickens. Add tofu and parsley, stir gently over heat until heated through.
Makes 4.

ASPARAGUS TIMBALES

Serve timbales hot or cold; they are best made just before serving. Recipe unsuitable to freeze or microwave.

**500g fresh asparagus spears,
    chopped**
30g butter
1 medium onion, chopped
2 tablespoons wholemeal plain flour
1 cup grated tasty cheese
4 eggs, lightly beaten
**½ large vegetable stock cube,
    crumbled**
pinch ground nutmeg

Boil, steam or microwave asparagus until tender; drain. Melt butter in small frying pan, add onion, stir over medium heat about 2 minutes or until onion is soft. Stir in flour, stir over medium heat 1 minute, transfer to large bowl.

Blend or process asparagus until smooth; add to bowl with cheese, eggs, stock cube and nutmeg, mix well. Pour mixture into 6 greased timbale moulds (½ cup capacity), cover each mould with foil. Place moulds in baking dish, pour in enough boiling water to come half way up sides of moulds. Bake in moderately slow oven for about 45 minutes or until set.
Makes 6.

HERBED TOMATOES WITH CRACKED WHEAT

Filling can be made up to a day ahead; keep, covered, in refrigerator. Recipe unsuitable to freeze or microwave.

¼ cup pine nuts
½ cup cracked wheat
1 medium zucchini, grated
1 tablespoon chopped fresh mint
3 teaspoons chopped fresh oregano
2 green shallots, chopped
2 tablespoons lemon juice
2 tablespoons oil
8 medium tomatoes

Toast nuts on oven tray in moderate oven for about 5 minutes, cool. Place wheat in small bowl, cover with boiling water, stand for 15 minutes. Drain in fine strainer, rinse well under cold water, dry as much as possible using absorbent paper.

Place wheat in medium bowl, stir in nuts, zucchini, mint, oregano, shallots, juice and oil. Cut base from tomatoes, scoop out flesh. Chop flesh, add to wheat mixture. Spoon mixture into tomatoes, replace lids.
Serves 4.

MARINATED BEAN SPROUT AND SESAME SALAD

Recipe can be made 2 hours ahead; keep, covered, in refrigerator. Recipe unsuitable to freeze.

¼ cup sesame seeds
500g bean sprouts
1 medium red pepper, sliced
1 medium green pepper, sliced
DRESSING
2 tablespoons olive oil
¼ cup lemon juice
2 tablespoons cider vinegar
2 teaspoons light soy sauce

Stir seeds over heat in small heavy-based frying pan until lightly browned. Combine seeds, sprouts and peppers in large bowl, pour over dressing; toss well, cover, refrigerate for about 2 hours, tossing occasionally.

Dressing: Combine all ingredients in a jar, shake well.

Serves 4.

SPICY VEGETABLES IN CRISPY BASKETS

Baskets can be made a day ahead; keep in airtight container. Assemble recipe just before serving. Recipe unsuitable to freeze or microwave.

4 sheets fillo pastry
¼ cup oil
SPICY VEGETABLES
1 tablespoon oil
1 small onion, sliced
1 clove garlic, crushed
1 small fresh red chilli, chopped
1 medium red pepper, chopped
1 medium carrot, sliced
350g broccoli, chopped
125g snow peas
2 teaspoons light soy sauce
2 tablespoons chopped fresh chives
½ cup water
2 teaspoons cornflour
1 tablespoon water, extra

Oil the outside of 4 ovenproof dishes (1 cup capacity). Place the dishes upside down onto lightly greased oven tray. Cut pastry sheets in half crossways, place 2 sheets on bench. Cover remaining pastry with greaseproof paper, then a damp cloth to prevent drying. Brush 1 sheet of pastry with oil, top with another sheet of pastry, brush with oil, place over a prepared dish, trim edges. Repeat with remaining pastry. Bake in moderate oven for about 5 minutes or until lightly browned; cool. Carefully remove pastry cases from dishes. Fill cases with vegetables.

Spicy Vegetables: Heat oil in wok or frying pan, add onion, garlic and chilli, stir-fry 1 minute, or until onion is soft. Add pepper, carrot, broccoli and snow peas, stir-fry for 1 minute. Add sauce, chives and water, stir-fry for 2 minutes. Blend cornflour with extra water, add to wok, stir until mixture boils and thickens slightly.

Serves 4.

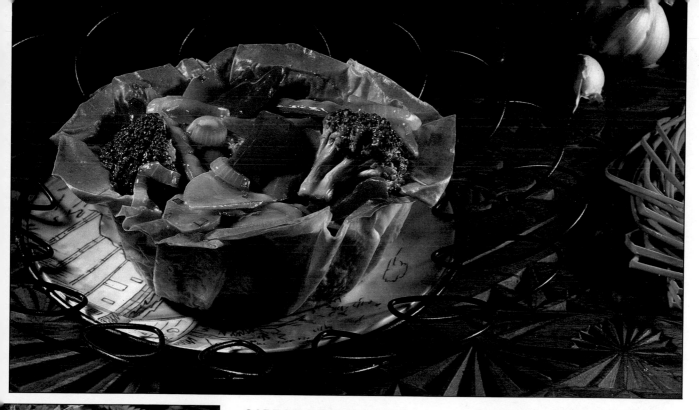

CARROT, AVOCADO AND SPROUT SALAD

Salad without avocado can be prepared several hours ahead; keep, covered, in refrigerator. Add avocado and dressing just before serving. Recipe unsuitable to freeze.

2½ cups (150g) bean sprouts
2 medium carrots, grated
1 tablespoon sunflower seed kernels
2 tablespoons chopped fresh parsley
1 medium avocado, sliced
HONEY DRESSING
2 tablespoons olive oil
2 tablespoons lemon juice
1 tablespoon honey
1 clove garlic, crushed

Combine sprouts, carrots, kernels and parsley in medium bowl. Pour over dressing, toss well; top with avocado.
Honey Dressing: Combine all ingredients in jar; shake well.
Serves 4.

ENDIVE AND PAPAW SALAD

Salad is best prepared close to serving time. Recipe unsuitable to freeze.

5 cups (½ bunch) chopped endive
1 small papaw, chopped
4 green shallots, chopped
1 large avocado, chopped
LIME AND GINGER DRESSING
¼ cup olive oil
¼ cup lime juice
1 tablespoon grated fresh ginger
¼ teaspoon curry powder

Combine endive, papaw, shallots and avocado in large bowl. Add dressing, toss gently to combine.
Lime and Ginger Dressing: Combine all ingredients in jar, shake well.
Serves 4.

ZUCCHINI AND FETA CHEESE SOUFFLES

Soufflés must be made just before serving. This recipe is not suitable to freeze or microwave.

1 medium zucchini, grated
salt
45g butter
¼ cup plain white flour
¼ teaspoon dry mustard
1 cup milk
125g feta cheese, crumbled
1 tablespoon grated parmesan cheese
4 eggs, separated

Place zucchini into colander, sprinkle with salt; toss lightly, stand over a bowl for 30 minutes to drain. Rinse zucchini under cold water, drain, squeeze out excess liquid.

Melt butter in medium saucepan, stir in flour and mustard, stir over medium heat for 1 minute (or microwave on HIGH for 1 minute). Remove from heat, gradually stir in milk, stir over high heat (or microwave on HIGH for about 3 minutes) until mixture boils and thickens; remove from heat, transfer to large bowl, stir in cheeses, zucchini and egg yolks.

Beat egg whites in medium bowl until soft peaks form, fold into zucchini mixture in 2 batches. Pour mixture into 4 ovenproof dishes (1 cup capacity). Place dishes on oven tray, bake in moderate oven for about 25 minutes or until golden brown.
Serves 4.

From left: Carrot, Avocado and Sprout Salad; Endive and Papaw Salad. ABOVE: Spicy Vegetables in Crispy Baskets.

Tray and plate: The Antique General Store (above); bowls: Shop 3, Balmain (left)

BUCKWHEAT CREPES WITH SPICY GREEN BEAN FILLING

Unfilled crêpes can be made 2 days ahead; keep, layered with greaseproof paper, in refrigerator. Crêpes can be frozen for 2 months. Filling is best prepared close to serving time. Recipe unsuitable to microwave.

BUCKWHEAT CREPES
½ cup wholemeal plain flour
½ cup buckwheat flour
1 egg, lightly beaten
1½ cups milk
15g butter
100g oyster mushrooms
SPICY GREEN BEAN FILLING
300g green beans
2 teaspoons oil
1 medium onion, chopped
2 cloves garlic, crushed
1 small red pepper, chopped
2 teaspoons garam masala
2 teaspoons ground cumin
½ teaspoon ground turmeric
¼ teaspoon chilli powder
5 medium tomatoes, peeled
1 tablespoon tomato paste
½ cup canned drained corn kernels
½ cup plain yoghurt

Buckwheat Crêpes: Sift flours into medium bowl, make well in centre, gradually stir in combined egg and milk, mix to a smooth batter (or blend or process all ingredients until smooth). Cover, stand for 30 minutes.

Pour 2 to 3 tablespoons of batter into heated greased heavy-based small frying pan; cook until lightly browned underneath. Turn crêpe, brown on other side. Repeat with remaining batter. You will need 12 crêpes for this recipe. Divide filling between crêpes, fold crêpes into quarters.

Melt butter in small frying pan, add mushrooms, stir over medium heat for about 3 minutes or until tender. Serve with crêpes.

Spicy Green Bean Filling: Cut beans lengthways into strips, then cut in half, boil, steam or microwave until tender. Heat oil in medium saucepan, add onion, garlic and pepper, stir over medium heat for about 2 minutes or until onion is soft.

Add spices, tomatoes, paste and corn, bring to boil, reduce heat, cover, simmer for 10 minutes. Add beans, stir until heated through. Remove from heat, gradually stir in yoghurt.

Serves 6.

BELOW: Buckwheat Crêpes with Spicy Bean Filling. LEFT: Zucchini and Feta Cheese Soufflés.

Plate: Made Where; basket and frying pan: The Country Trader (below); board: Shop 3, Balmain (left)

POLENTA AND HERB SEASONED ARTICHOKES

Artichokes can be prepared several hours ahead; keep, covered, in refrigerator. Recipe unsuitable to freeze or microwave.

4 medium artichokes
2 teaspoons oil
2 sticks celery, chopped
2 tablespoons chopped fresh chives
2 tablespoons chopped fresh sage
⅔ cup stale wholemeal breadcrumbs
⅓ cup polenta
½ cup roasted unsalted cashew nuts, chopped
1 egg, lightly beaten
¼ cup lemon juice

LEMON SAGE SAUCE
1 cup water
⅓ cup lemon juice
1 tablespoon chopped fresh sage
3 teaspoons light soy sauce
1 tablespoon cornflour
2 tablespoons water, extra

Cut base from artichokes so they sit flat. Remove the tough outer leaves, and shorten the remaining leaves with scissors.

Heat oil in small frying pan, add celery, chives and sage, stir over medium heat until celery is soft; stir in breadcrumbs, polenta and nuts, stir over heat further minute. Remove from heat; cool. Stir in egg.

Starting from outside of each artichoke, press seasoning between leaves until artichokes are packed tightly. Place in single layer in baking dish, pour over lemon juice, bake, uncovered, in moderate oven about 40 minutes or until artichokes are tender; brush occasionally with juice during cooking. Serve topped with sauce.

Lemon Sage Sauce: Combine water, juice, sage and sauce in small saucepan, bring to boil, reduce heat, simmer, uncovered, 5 minutes.

Blend cornflour with extra water, add to pan, stir over high heat until sauce boils and thickens.

Serves 4.

Polenta and Herb Seasoned Artichokes.

Main Courses

Meals to remember are built around dishes like these. We dressed vegetables with flair and made them more tempting than ever before. And we used nuts, beans, pastry, pasta, cheese and more in lots of healthy, tasty ways you will enjoy. Some can also be served as entrées, if you like; others would make delicious party fare.

ABOVE: Honeyed Cabbage and Pineapple Stir-Fry.

HONEYED CABBAGE AND PINEAPPLE STIR-FRY

Stir fry is best made close to serving time. This recipe is not suitable to freeze or microwave.

1 large kumara
1 tablespoon oil
1 medium onion, quartered
½ small cabbage, shredded
4 cups (250g) bean sprouts
1 medium red pepper, sliced
440g can unsweetened pineapple
   pieces, drained
1 tablespoon hoisin sauce
1 tablespoon light soy sauce
1 tablespoon honey

Cut kumara into 5cm sticks; boil, steam or microwave until just tender.

Heat oil in large frying pan or wok, add onion, stir over medium heat for about 2 minutes or until onion is soft. Add cabbage, sprouts and pepper to pan, stir over medium heat further 2 minutes. Stir in pineapple with combined sauces and honey. Stir over heat further minute.

Serves 4.

PUMPKIN PASTA WITH FRESH VEGETABLE SAUCE

You will need to cook about 200g pumpkin for this recipe. Recipe is best prepared just before serving. Pasta can be frozen for 2 months. Sauce unsuitable to freeze or microwave.

PUMPKIN PASTA
1¾ cups white plain flour
2 eggs
½ cup cold mashed cooked pumpkin
FRESH VEGETABLE SAUCE
1 medium carrot
2 medium zucchini
2 tablespoons oil
1 medium onion, chopped
1 medium red pepper, sliced
1 tablespoon wholemeal plain flour
2 medium tomatoes, peeled, chopped
1 teaspoon chopped fresh marjoram
1 teaspoon chopped fresh basil
2 teaspoons tomato paste
1 teaspoon brown sugar
1 cup water
½ large vegetable stock cube, crumbled

Pumpkin Pasta: Process flour, eggs and pumpkin until mixture is well combined and forms a ball. Turn dough onto lightly floured surface, knead for 5 minutes. Wrap dough in plastic wrap, refrigerate for 30 minutes. Divide dough into 4 portions. Place 1 portion on bench, cover remaining dough with plastic wrap to prevent drying out.

Roll dough on lightly floured surface to a rectangle 2mm thick, sprinkle lightly with flour, roll up firmly from a narrow end. Cut dough into 8mm slices, unroll strips, place onto tray to dry for about 15 minutes. Repeat with remaining dough. Add pasta gradually to large saucepan of boiling water, boil, uncovered, for 4 minutes; drain. Serve with sauce.

Fresh Vegetable Sauce: Cut carrot and zucchini into thin strips. Heat oil in large frying pan, add onion and carrot, stir over medium heat for about 3 minutes or until onion is soft. Add zucchini and pepper, stir over medium heat for 3 minutes. Stir in flour, stir over medium heat further minute.

Stir in tomatoes, marjoram, basil, paste, sugar, water and stock cube, stir over high heat until mixture boils and thickens slightly, cover, reduce heat, simmer for about 7 minutes or until vegetables are tender.

Serves 4.

From left: Pumpkin Pasta with Fresh Vegetable Sauce; Wholemeal Ravioli with Eggplant Filling.

WHOLEMEAL RAVIOLI WITH EGGPLANT FILLING

Ravioli can be made 2 days ahead; keep, covered, in refrigerator or freeze for up to 2 months. Ravioli dough can be rolled using a pasta machine: follow manufacturer's directions. Recipe unsuitable to microwave.

RAVIOLI
2 cups wholemeal plain flour
2 eggs, lightly beaten
2 tablespoons oil
⅓ cup water
2 tablespoons chopped fresh parsley
½ cup grated parmesan cheese
EGGPLANT FILLING
1 medium eggplant, chopped
1 medium zucchini, chopped
salt
30g butter
1 medium onion, chopped
100g ricotta cheese
1 egg, lightly beaten
2 tablespoons chopped fresh parsley

STEP 1
Ravioli: Process flour, eggs, oil and water until mixture forms a ball.

STEP 2
Turn dough onto lightly floured surface, knead for 5 minutes. Wrap dough in plastic wrap, refrigerate for 30 minutes. Divide dough into 4 portions. Place 1 portion on bench, cover remaining dough with plastic wrap to prevent drying out. Roll dough out to 2mm thickness on lightly floured surface, cut into 2 x 14cm strips.

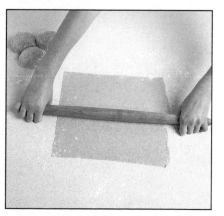

STEP 3
Cover 1 dough strip with tea-towel to prevent drying out. Place heaped teaspoons of filling at 1½cm intervals on 1 strip of dough.

STEP 4
Lightly brush edges and between mounds of filling with water, top with a second dough strip, press edges together to seal.

STEP 5
Cut between mounds of filling using knife or fluted pastry cutter. Repeat with remaining dough and filling. Add ravioli gradually to large saucepan of boiling water, boil, uncovered, for about 8 minutes or until tender; drain. Serve sprinkled with parsley and parmesan cheese.

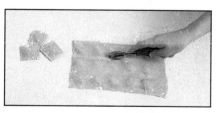

Eggplant Filling: Place eggplant and zucchini in colander, sprinkle with salt, stand for 30 minutes, rinse under cold water; drain. Melt butter in large frying pan, add onion, stir over medium heat for about 3 minutes or until onion is soft. Add eggplant and zucchini, stir over medium heat for about 5 minutes or until eggplant is soft; cool to room temperature. Blend or process eggplant mixture until smooth, transfer mixture to medium bowl. Add ricotta cheese, egg and parsley, stir well.
Serves 4.

LETTUCE ROLLS WITH BEETROOT SALAD

Make rolls close to serving time. Salad can be made a day ahead. Recipe unsuitable to freeze.

1 medium carrot, chopped
200g yellow baby squash, chopped
½ cup fresh or frozen peas
1 medium cucumber, chopped
1 medium tomato, chopped
6 green shallots, chopped
¼ cup plain yoghurt
2 teaspoons tamari shoyu
¼ teaspoon sesame oil
1 teaspoon grated lemon rind
1 clove garlic, crushed
1 tablespoon chopped fresh mint
12 large lettuce leaves
BEETROOT SALAD
4 medium beetroot
1 tablespoon olive oil
1 tablespoon raspberry vinegar
1 tablespoon chopped fresh parsley

Boil, steam or microwave carrot, squash and peas until tender; place in large bowl. Add cucumber, tomato and shallots with combined yoghurt, tamari shoyu, oil, rind, garlic and mint; mix well. Drop lettuce leaves into large saucepan of boiling water, drain immediately. Place leaves into a bowl of iced water, drain on absorbent paper. Spoon filling evenly onto centre of each leaf, wrap securely. Serve rolls with beetroot salad.

Beetroot Salad: Cover beetroot with water in large saucepan, bring to boil, reduce heat, cover, simmer for about 30 minutes or until tender, drain; cool. Peel beetroot, slice thickly. Place into medium bowl, add combined oil, vinegar and parsley.

Serves 4.

CAULIFLOWER AND CELERY PIES

Filling can be made a day ahead; keep, covered, in refrigerator. Recipe unsuitable to freeze.

PASTRY
1 cup wholemeal plain flour
¼ cup oat bran
90g butter
2 tablespoons water, approximately
1 egg, lightly beaten
2 tablespoons sesame seeds
CAULIFLOWER CELERY FILLING
½ small cauliflower, chopped
30g butter
1 medium onion, thinly sliced
2 sticks celery, thinly sliced
¼ cup white plain flour
2¼ cups water
1 large vegetable stock cube, crumbled
3 teaspoons seeded mustard

Pastry: Combine flour and oat bran in medium bowl, rub in butter. Add enough water to mix to a firm dough (pastry can also be made in food processor). Cover, refrigerate 30 minutes. Roll pastry between 2 sheets of plastic wrap or greaseproof paper until about 5mm thick.

Spoon filling into 6 ovenproof dishes (¾ cup capacity), brush edges of dishes with egg. Cut pastry into 6 rounds large enough to cover dishes, press firmly around edges then decorate with fork, if desired. Brush pastry with remaining egg, sprinkle with sesame seeds. Bake in moderately hot oven for about 20 minutes or until pastry is well browned.

Cauliflower Celery Filling: Boil, steam or microwave cauliflower until just tender, drain.

Melt butter in large saucepan, add onion and celery, stir over medium heat for about 2 minutes (or microwave on HIGH for about 3 minutes) or until onion is soft. Stir in flour, stir over medium heat further minute (or microwave on HIGH for 1 minute). Remove from heat, gradually stir in combined water, stock cube and mustard, stir over high heat (or microwave on HIGH for about 5 minutes) until mixture boils and thickens; add cauliflower.

Serves 6.

BELOW: Cauliflower and Celery Pies.
LEFT: Lettuce Rolls with Beetroot Salad.

Chair & basket: Mid-City Home and Garden; table & spoon: The Country Trader; cloth: Casa Shopping (below); plate: The Bay Tree (left)

CHEESY NUT LOAF WITH TOMATO SAUCE

Loaf and sauce can be made a day ahead; keep, covered, in refrigerator. You will need to cook ⅓ cup brown rice for this recipe. This recipe is unsuitable to freeze.

1 tablespoon oil
1 medium onion, chopped
1 medium green pepper, chopped
1 medium tomato, chopped
1 cup roasted unsalted cashew nuts
1 cup blanched almonds
1 medium carrot, grated
1 cup cooked brown rice
¾ cup grated tasty cheese
1 egg, lightly beaten
TOMATO SAUCE
1 tablespoon oil
6 medium tomatoes, chopped
¼ cup water

Lightly oil 14cm x 21cm loaf pan, line base with greaseproof paper. Heat oil in small saucepan, add onion, pepper and tomato, stir over low heat for about 4 minutes (or microwave on HIGH for about 3 minutes) or until pepper is tender; cool. Blend or process cashews and almonds until finely chopped.

Combine onion mixture, nuts, carrot, rice, cheese and egg in a large bowl, mix well. Press mixture evenly into prepared pan, bake in moderate oven for about 40 minutes or until lightly browned. Serve with sauce.

Tomato Sauce: Heat oil in medium saucepan, add tomatoes, cook over low heat 10 minutes (or microwave on HIGH 6 minutes). Blend or process tomatoes and water until smooth, strain; reheat before serving.

Serves 4.

SPINACH AND MUSHROOM TIMBALES

Cook timbales close to serving time. This recipe is not suitable to freeze or microwave.

SPINACH LAYER
1 bunch (40 leaves) English spinach
1 egg
pinch nutmeg
2 tablespoons milk
MUSHROOM LAYER
30g butter
1 clove garlic, crushed
1 medium onion, finely chopped
250g mushrooms, sliced
1½ tablespoons wholemeal plain flour
½ cup milk
2 eggs, lightly beaten
GARLIC AND CHIVE SAUCE
2 teaspoons butter
1 clove garlic, crushed
1½ teaspoons white plain flour
½ cup milk
1 tablespoon chopped fresh chives

Lightly grease 4 ovenproof dishes (¾ cup capacity). Spoon spinach layer evenly into dishes, top with mushroom layer; cover dishes with foil. Place dishes in baking dish, pour in enough boiling water to come halfway up sides of dishes. Bake in moderate oven for about 1 hour or until set. Stand for 5 minutes before turning onto serving plates. Serve with sauce.

Spinach Layer: Boil, steam or microwave spinach until tender; drain well. Blend spinach, egg, nutmeg and milk until smooth.

Mushroom Layer: Melt butter in medium saucepan, add garlic and onion, stir over medium heat for about 2 minutes (or microwave on HIGH for about 3 minutes) or until onion is soft.

Add mushrooms, stir over medium heat for 2 minutes (or microwave on HIGH for 2 minutes). Stir in flour, stir over medium heat for 1 minute (or microwave on HIGH for 1 minute). Remove from heat, gradually stir in milk, stir over high heat (or microwave on HIGH for 2 minutes) until mixture boils and thickens. Cool slightly for 5 minutes; stir in eggs.

Garlic and Chive Sauce: Melt butter with garlic in small saucepan (or microwave on HIGH about 30 seconds). Stir in flour, stir over medium heat for 30 seconds (or microwave on HIGH for about 30 seconds). Remove from heat, gradually stir in milk, stir over high heat (or microwave on HIGH for about 1 minute) until mixture boils and thickens. Strain sauce, stir in chives.

Serves 4.

BRAZIL NUT CUTLETS WITH PIMIENTO SAUCE

Cutlets can be made a day ahead; keep, covered, in refrigerator. Cooked cutlets and sauce can be frozen for up to a month. This recipe is not suitable to microwave.

2 cups (310g) brazil nuts, finely chopped
1 cup stale wholemeal breadcrumbs
2 tablespoons chopped fresh parsley
2 eggs, lightly beaten
2 tablespoons oil

PIMIENTO SAUCE
200g can pimientos, drained
1 large vegetable stock cube, crumbled
¼ cup water
¼ cup chopped fresh parsley

Combine nuts, breadcrumbs, parsley and eggs in medium bowl; mix well. Divide mixture into 8 portions, shape into cutlets or patties; refrigerate for 30 minutes. Heat oil in large frying pan, add cutlets, cook over medium heat for 2 minutes on each side or until golden brown. Serve with sauce.

Pimiento Sauce: Blend or process pimientos, stock cube and water until smooth; pour into small saucepan. Stir over medium heat for about 2 minutes (or microwave on high for about 2 minutes). Stir in parsley.

Makes 8.

ABOVE: From left: Brazil Nut Cutlets with Pimiento Sauce; Cheesy Nut Loaf with Tomato Sauce. LEFT: Spinach and Mushroom Timbales.

Plates and box: Made Where; table: Country Furniture Antiques; screen: Corso de Fiori

CARROT PARCELS WITH BASIL SAUCE

You will need to grate about 4 medium carrots for this recipe. Recipe unsuitable to freeze or microwave.

30g butter
1 small leek, sliced
3 cups grated carrot
250g ricotta cheese
2 tablespoons chopped fresh parsley
2 tablespoons sunflower seed kernels
1 egg, lightly beaten
6 sheets fillo pastry
45g butter, melted, extra
1 tablespoon packaged breadcrumbs
BASIL SAUCE
15g butter
1 clove garlic, crushed
1 tablespoon wholemeal plain flour
¾ cup milk
½ cup cream
2 tablespoons chopped fresh basil
1 tablespoon grated parmesan cheese

BELOW: Carrot Parcels with Basil Sauce.
RIGHT: From top: Chilli Vegetable Hot Pot; Potato-Crusted Lentil Hot Pot.

Tiles: Country Floors (below); pot and tin: Country Form; enamel dish: Oldentime Antiques; spoon: Corso de Fiori (right)

Melt butter in small saucepan, add leek, stir over medium heat for about 3 minutes (or microwave on HIGH for about 3 minutes) or until leek is soft. Combine leek, carrot, cheese, parsley, kernels and egg in large bowl.

Cut pastry sheets in half crossways, place 3 pastry sheets on bench, cover remaining pastry with greaseproof paper, then a damp cloth to prevent drying out. Layer the 3 pastry sheets together, brushing each sheet with the extra butter.

Place quarter of the carrot mixture along short end of pastry, fold in sides and roll up like a Swiss roll. Repeat with remaining pastry, extra butter and carrot mixture.

Place parcels on greased oven tray, brush with extra butter, sprinkle with breadcrumbs. Bake in moderate oven for about 30 minutes or until golden brown. Serve with basil sauce.

Basil Sauce: Melt butter with garlic in medium saucepan (or microwave on HIGH for 30 seconds). Stir in flour, stir over medium heat for 1 minute (or microwave on HIGH for 1 minute). Remove from heat, gradually stir in combined milk and cream, stir over high heat (or microwave on HIGH for about 2 minutes) until mixture boils and thickens. Remove from heat, stir in basil and cheese.

Makes 4.

CHILLI VEGETABLE HOT POT

Recipe can be prepared 3 hours ahead; keep, covered, in refrigerator. This recipe is not suitable to freeze or microwave.

2 tablespoons olive oil
1 clove garlic, crushed
1 small fresh red chilli, chopped
2 medium Spanish red onions, chopped
2 medium carrots, chopped
2 medium red peppers, chopped
425g can tomatoes
½ cup water
1 tablespoon tomato paste
½ teaspoon ground cumin
310g can red kidney beans, drained
90g mushrooms, sliced
2 tablespoons chopped fresh parsley

Heat oil in medium frying pan, add garlic, chilli and onions, stir occasionally over low heat for about 15 minutes or until onions are soft. Add carrots and peppers, stir for 1 minute. Add undrained crushed tomatoes, water, paste and cumin, bring to boil, reduce heat, cover, simmer for about 10 minutes. Add beans and mushrooms, simmer for 5 minutes. Sprinkle with parsley before serving.

Serves 4.

POTATO-CRUSTED LENTIL HOT POT

Hot pot is best prepared close to serving time. Recipe unsuitable to freeze or microwave.

¾ cup red lentils
5 medium potatoes
1 tablespoon oil
2 medium onions, chopped
2 medium carrots, chopped
3 sticks celery, chopped
3 cloves garlic, crushed
1 teaspoon curry powder
5 medium ripe tomatoes, peeled, chopped
1 large vegetable stock cube, crumbled
1 cup water
2 tablespoons tomato paste
2 tablespoons chopped fresh parsley
15g butter, melted
¼ teaspoon paprika

Add lentils to large saucepan of boiling water, bring to boil, reduce heat, simmer, uncovered, for 10 minutes; drain well. Boil, steam or microwave potatoes in their skins until tender.

Heat oil in large saucepan, add onions, carrots, celery and garlic, stir over medium heat for about 5 minutes or until onions are soft. Stir in curry powder, cook for 1 minute. Add tomatoes, stock cube, water and paste, bring to boil, reduce heat, cover, simmer for 10 minutes. Stir in parsley and lentils; spoon into large ovenproof dish (8 cup capacity).

Slice potatoes, arrange over lentil mixture. Brush potatoes with butter, sprinkle with paprika. Bake in moderate oven for about 45 minutes or until lightly browned.

Serves 4.

FRUITY SEASONED PEPPERS

Prepare peppers close to serving time. Recipe unsuitable to freeze.

2 medium carrots, grated
2 medium zucchini, grated
½ cup chopped pitted prunes
4 green shallots, chopped
125g feta cheese, chopped
4 medium red peppers
ORANGE MAYONNAISE
⅓ cup mayonnaise
2 tablespoons orange juice

Combine carrots, zucchini, prunes and shallots in medium bowl, add mayonnaise; mix well. Add cheese and mix lightly. Cut each pepper in half crossways, remove seeds and any membranes. Fill each pepper half with carrot mixture.

Orange Mayonnaise: Combine mayonnaise and orange juice in small bowl; mix well.

Serves 4.

ABOVE: Leek Roulade with Ricotta Corn Filling. RIGHT: From top: Fruity Seasoned Peppers; Avocado and Garbanzo Salad.

Plate, knife and fork: Made Where (above); box: Country Form (right)

LEEK ROULADE WITH RICOTTA CORN FILLING

Roulade is best made close to serving time. This recipe is not suitable to freeze or microwave.

30g butter
1 medium leek, sliced
1 clove garlic, crushed
60g butter, extra
⅓ cup white plain flour
1 cup milk
4 eggs, separated
2 tablespoons grated parmesan cheese
RICOTTA CORN FILLING
100g ricotta cheese
2 x 130g cans corn kernels, drained
⅓ cup chopped fresh chives

Grease 25cm x 30cm Swiss roll pan, line base with paper, grease paper. Melt butter in medium saucepan, add leek and garlic, stir over medium heat for about 5 minutes (or microwave on HIGH for about 5 minutes) or until leek is soft.

Melt extra butter in medium saucepan, stir in flour, stir over medium heat for 1 minute (or microwave on HIGH for 1 minute). Remove from heat, gradually stir in milk, stir over high heat (or microwave on HIGH for about 2 minutes) until mixture boils and thickens. Stir in egg yolks and leek mixture, transfer mixture to large bowl.

Beat egg whites in medium bowl with electric mixer until soft peaks form, fold lightly into leek mixture. Spread mixture into prepared pan. Bake in hot oven about 12 minutes or until puffed and golden brown. Sprinkle clean tea-towel evenly with parmesan cheese. Turn roulade onto tea-towel, carefully remove lining paper, spread roulade evenly with filling. Holding tea-towel with both hands, gently lift and roll roulade from a wide side. Serve warm.

Ricotta Corn Filling: Beat cheese in small bowl with electric mixer until smooth, stir in corn and chives.

Serves 4 to 6.

AVOCADO AND GARBANZO SALAD

Salad can be made a day ahead; keep, covered, in refrigerator. Recipe unsuitable to freeze.

200g yellow squash, chopped
200g can pimientos, drained
425g can garbanzos, drained,
1 small onion, thinly sliced
1 medium avocado, chopped
½ cup stuffed green olives
CHILLI DRESSING
¼ cup olive oil
¼ cup lemon juice
2 small fresh red chillies, finely chopped
¼ teaspoon sugar

Boil, steam or microwave squash until just tender, drain, rinse under cold water, drain. Cut pimientos into thin strips. Combine squash, pimientos, garbanzos, onion, avocado and olives in large bowl, add dressing, toss gently until combined.

Chilli Dressing: Combine all ingredients in jar, shake well.

Serves 4.

SPICY GARBANZO AND VEGETABLE HOT POT

Recipe can be made a day ahead; keep, covered, in refrigerator. Recipe unsuitable to freeze.

2 tablespoons oil
1 medium onion, chopped
1 clove garlic, crushed
1 tablespoon curry powder
1 teaspoon ground cumin
¼ teaspoon ground cardamom
¼ teaspoon ground nutmeg
pinch ground allspice
1 small fresh red chilli, finely chopped
1 tablespoon finely chopped fresh ginger
1 tablespoon wholemeal plain flour
2 cups water
1 large vegetable stock cube, crumbled
2 medium carrots, chopped
2 medium potatoes, chopped
½ small cauliflower, chopped
250g green beans, chopped
1 medium apple, peeled, chopped
425g can garbanzos, drained
200g carton plain yoghurt
1 tablespoon chopped fresh coriander
¼ cup chopped roasted cashew nuts

Heat oil in large saucepan, add onion, stir over medium heat for about 2 minutes (or microwave on HIGH for about 3 minutes) or until onion is soft. Add garlic, curry powder, spices, chilli and ginger, stir over medium heat for 1 minute (or microwave on HIGH for 1 minute). Stir in flour, stir over high heat for 1 minute (or microwave on HIGH for 1 minute).

Remove from heat, gradually stir in combined water and stock cube, stir over high heat (or microwave on HIGH) until mixture boils and thickens slightly. Add carrots, potatoes, cauliflower and beans, cover, simmer for about 10 minutes (or microwave on HIGH for about 8 minutes) or until vegetables are tender.

Add apple, garbanzos, yoghurt and coriander, stir over medium heat until heated through. Sprinkle with nuts before serving.
Serves 4.

EGGPLANT CASSEROLE

Casserole can be prepared a day ahead; keep, covered, in refrigerator. This recipe is not suitable to freeze or microwave.

1 large eggplant
1 tablespoon cider vinegar
2 tablespoons skim milk
¼ cup wholemeal plain flour
1 tablespoon sesame seeds
¼ cup oil
100g mushrooms, sliced
3 medium tomatoes, sliced
1 tablespoon chopped fresh basil
1 cup stale wholemeal breadcrumbs
¼ cup grated parmesan cheese
2 medium zucchini, grated
2 green shallots, chopped
30g butter, melted

Cut eggplant into 1cm slices, place in large bowl, cover with boiling water, add vinegar, stand for 15 minutes; drain, pat dry with absorbent paper. Dip slices in milk then in combined flour and sesame seeds.

Heat half the oil in large frying pan, add half the eggplant in single layer, cook for about 2 minutes on each side or until lightly browned; drain on absorbent paper. Repeat with remaining oil and eggplant. Place half the eggplant in shallow ovenproof dish (6 cup capacity), top with mushrooms and tomatoes, sprinkle with basil.

Combine breadcrumbs and cheese in small bowl, sprinkle half the mixture over tomatoes. Top with combined zucchini and shallots, cover with remaining eggplant, then sprinkle with remaining breadcrumb mixture. Drizzle with butter, bake in moderate oven for about 30 minutes or until golden.
Serves 4.

From top: Spicy Garbanzo and Vegetable Hot Pot; Eggplant Casserole.

Ceramic dishes: Villa Italiana; wooden screen: Corso de Fiori; rug: The Caspian Studio

BLACK-EYED BEAN CASSEROLE

Casserole can be made up to a day ahead; keep, covered, in refrigerator. This recipe is not suitable to freeze or microwave.

1½ cups (250g) black-eyed beans
425g can tomatoes
1 medium Spanish red onion, chopped
1 clove garlic, crushed
½ cup tomato paste
1 small green pepper, chopped
3 cups water
¼ cup chopped fresh parsley
¼ cup chopped fresh basil
500g baby mushrooms, sliced
310g can corn kernels, drained

Cover beans with cold water, stand overnight. Drain beans, place in medium saucepan with enough water to cover, bring to boil, boil for 30 minutes, drain.

Combine beans, undrained crushed tomatoes, onion, garlic, paste, pepper and water in a large saucepan. Bring to boil, reduce heat, cover, simmer for 1 hour, stirring occasionally, or until beans are tender. Add parsley, basil, mushrooms and corn, mix well, simmer further 15 minutes.

Serves 4 to 6.

PEANUT PATTIES WITH SPICY BARBECUE SAUCE

Peanut mixture can be made several hours ahead; keep, covered, in refrigerator. You will need to cook about ½ cup brown rice for this recipe. This recipe is not suitable to freeze or microwave.

1¼ cups (155g) unsalted roasted peanuts
1½ cups cooked brown rice
1 medium onion, chopped
2 eggs
2 tablespoons smooth peanut butter
2 tablespoons fruit chutney
1½ teaspoons curry powder
2 tablespoons oil

SPICY BARBECUE SAUCE
2 teaspoons cornflour
½ cup water
½ cup tomato sauce
2 teaspoons Worcestershire sauce
½ teaspoon tabasco sauce
1 tablespoon brown sugar

Blend or process peanuts and rice until finely chopped, add onion, eggs, peanut butter, chutney and curry powder; process until combined. Refrigerate mixture for at least 30 minutes.

Using lightly floured hands, shape mixture into 8 patties. Heat oil in large frying pan, add patties, cook for about 5 minutes or until browned on both sides; drain on absorbent paper. Serve with spicy barbecue sauce.

Spicy Barbecue Sauce: Blend cornflour with water in small saucepan, add remaining ingredients, stir over high heat (or microwave on HIGH for about 3 minutes) until mixture boils and thickens.

Makes 8.

POLENTA AND EGGPLANT WITH TOMATO SAUCE

Polenta and sauce can be made up to a day ahead; keep, covered, in refrigerator. Polenta and eggplant unsuitable to freeze. Sauce can be frozen for up to 2 months. Polenta and eggplant unsuitable to microwave.

1 litre (4 cups) water
1 cup polenta
¼ cup oil
1 medium eggplant
salt
white plain flour
oil for shallow-frying, extra
TOMATO SAUCE
2 teaspoons oil
1 medium red pepper, chopped
1 medium onion, chopped
1 clove garlic, crushed
1 teaspoon dried oregano leaves
425g can tomatoes
2 tablespoons tomato paste
¼ cup water

Lightly oil 19cm x 29cm lamington pan. Place water into large saucepan, bring to boil. Gradually sprinkle polenta into water; mix well. Cover, reduce heat to low; cook, stirring occasionally, for about 30 minutes or until polenta is very thick. Spread polenta evenly into prepared pan, cool; stand for 2 hours. Cut polenta into 12 pieces. Heat oil in a large frying pan, add polenta, cook for about 3 minutes each side or until golden; keep warm.

Cut eggplant into 1cm strips, place in colander, sprinkle with salt; stand for 30 minutes. Rinse eggplant under cold water, drain, pat dry with absorbent paper. Toss eggplant strips in flour; shake away excess flour. Shallow-fry strips in batches in hot extra oil until golden brown; drain on absorbent paper; keep warm.

Pour smooth sauce evenly into plates, top with polenta and eggplant, top with remaining sauce.

Tomato Sauce: Heat oil in large saucepan, add pepper, onion, garlic and oregano, stir over medium heat for about 2 minutes (or microwave on HIGH for 3 minutes) or until onion is soft. Add undrained crushed tomatoes, paste and water, cook over medium heat for about 20 minutes (or microwave on HIGH for about 10 minutes) or until vegetables are soft. Blend or process half sauce mixture until smooth.

Serves 4.

BELOW: From left: Vegetable Rissoles with Plum Sauce; Polenta and Eggplant with Tomato Sauce. LEFT: From left: Black-Eyed Bean Casserole; Peanut Patties with Spicy Barbecue Sauce.

Plates and basket: Corso de Fiori; napkin: The Australian East India Co (below); table: Country Form; buckets: The Parterre Garden (left)

VEGETABLE RISSOLES WITH PLUM SAUCE

Recipe can be made up to 3 days ahead; keep, covered, in refrigerator. This recipe is not suitable to freeze or microwave.

½ cup red lentils
1½ cups water
425g can garbanzos, drained
1 tablespoon oil
1 medium leek, finely sliced
1 medium carrot, grated
½ teaspoon ground cumin
½ teaspoon ground coriander
1 tablespoon chopped fresh mint
2 teaspoons lemon juice
¼ cup packaged breadcrumbs
¼ cup packaged breadcrumbs, extra
¼ cup flaked almonds, crushed
1 tablespoon oil, extra
PLUM SAUCE
1 teaspoon oil
1 medium onion, sliced
425g can dessert plums
1½ tablespoons light soy sauce
1 tablespoon castor sugar
1 teaspoon cornflour
¼ cup water

Place lentils and water in medium saucepan, bring to boil, reduce heat, cover, simmer for about 10 minutes or until lentils are soft, drain. Blend or process garbanzos until smooth.

Heat oil in large saucepan, add leek and carrot, stir over medium heat for about 3 minutes or until leek is soft. Add cumin, coriander, mint, juice and breadcrumbs. Add lentils and garbanzos to pan, mix well; cool.

Divide mixture into 8 portions, shape into rissoles, toss in combined extra breadcrumbs and almonds. Heat extra oil in large frying pan, add rissoles, cook over medium heat for about 5 minutes on each side or until golden brown. Serve with plum sauce.

Plum Sauce: Heat oil in small saucepan, add onion, cook over low heat for about 5 minutes or until soft. Drain plums, reserve ¼ cup of the syrup. Blend or process plums, reserved syrup, sauce and sugar until smooth, return to pan. Blend cornflour with water, add to pan, stir over high heat until mixture boils and thickens slightly.

Serves 4.

RIGHT: From top: Minted Sprout and Tempeh Salad; Fresh Herb Seasoned Eggs. FAR RIGHT: Vegetable Parcels with Yoghurt Sauce.

Plates Villa Italiana; cane basket; Mosmania; wreath: Made Where (far right); plates: Country Form (right)

MINTED SPROUT AND TEMPEH SALAD

Salad and dressing can be made several hours ahead; keep, covered, in refrigerator. Recipe is unsuitable to freeze or microwave.

1 tablespoon sesame seeds
½ x 300g packet tempeh, sliced
¼ cup cider vinegar
1 tablespoon grated fresh ginger
¼ cup tamari shoyu
wholemeal plain flour
1 egg, lightly beaten
¼ cup skim milk
1 cup stale wholemeal breadcrumbs
**1 cup finely chopped unsalted
   unroasted peanuts**
oil for shallow-frying
1 medium honeydew melon, chopped
1 medium green cucumber, chopped
4 green shallots, chopped
2 medium oranges
1 cup bean sprouts
DRESSING
200g carton plain yoghurt
2 tablespoons smooth peanut butter
1 tablespoon chopped fresh mint
1 tablespoon tamari shoyu
1 tablespoon lemon juice
1 tablespoon honey

Stir seeds over heat in heavy-based small frying pan until lightly browned, remove from pan to cool.

Combine tempeh, vinegar, ginger and tamari shoyu in small bowl, cover, refrigerate overnight.

Remove tempeh from marinade, drain on absorbent paper. Dust with flour, dip into combined egg and milk, then into combined breadcrumbs and peanuts. Shallow-fry tempeh in hot oil until golden brown; drain tempeh on absorbent paper.

Combine tempeh, melon, cucumber, shallots, orange segments and sprouts in a large bowl. Pour over dressing, sprinkle with sesame seeds just before serving.

Dressing: Combine all ingredients in small bowl; mix well.

Serves 4.

FRESH HERB SEASONED EGGS

Eggs can be hard-boiled a day ahead; keep, covered, in refrigerator. Seasoning is best prepared close to serving time. Recipe unsuitable to freeze or microwave.

8 hard-boiled eggs
8 cherry tomatoes, halved
1½ cups watercress springs
FRESH HERB SEASONING
¼ cup mayonnaise
1 tablespoon chopped fresh parsley
1 tablespoon chopped fresh chives
1 teaspoon chopped fresh thyme
**2 tablespoons grated parmesan
   cheese**

Cut eggs in half crossways, reserve yolks for seasoning. Place seasoning into piping bag fitted with large fluted tube, pipe mixture into egg halves. Serve with tomatoes and watercress.

Fresh Herb Seasoning: Push reserved yolks through fine strainer into medium bowl, stir in remaining ingredients.

Serves 4.

VEGETABLE PARCELS WITH YOGHURT SAUCE

Parcels can be prepared a day ahead; keep, covered, in refrigerator. Recipe unsuitable to freeze or microwave.

⅓ cup oil
¼ teaspoon black mustard seeds
**1 tablespoon finely chopped
   fresh ginger**
1 medium onion, finely chopped
¼ teaspoon ground turmeric
¼ teaspoon chilli powder
1 teaspoon ground cumin
2 teaspoons ground coriander
½ teaspoon garam masala
¼ teaspoon Vecon
4 medium carrots, chopped
1 cup frozen peas
½ cup chopped fresh coriander
¼ cup water
8 sheets fillo pastry
¼ cup oil, extra

YOGHURT SAUCE
½ cup plain yoghurt
¼ cup mango chutney
**2 teaspoons chopped fresh
   coriander**

Heat oil in large saucepan, add seeds, stir over medium heat until seeds begin to crack. Add ginger and onion, stir over medium heat for about 2 minutes or until onion is soft. Stir in turmeric, chilli, cumin, ground coriander, garam masala and Vecon, cook for 1 minute. Add carrots, peas, fresh coriander and water to pan, cover, cook over low heat for about 20 minutes or until vegetables are tender, stirring occasionally; cool.

Brush 1 sheet of pastry with extra oil, top with another sheet of pastry, brush with oil. Place a quarter of mixture along short side of pastry, leaving 5cm border, fold sides in, roll up like a Swiss roll. Brush all over with more extra oil, place onto oven tray. Repeat with remaining pastry and filling. Bake in moderate oven for about 30 minutes or until lightly browned. Serve with yoghurt sauce.

Yoghurt Sauce: Combine all ingredients in small bowl.

Makes 4.

WHOLEMEAL SPINACH AND RICOTTA CREPES

Recipe can be prepared several hours ahead; keep, covered, in refrigerator. Bake just before serving. Crepes can be frozen for up to 2 months.

CREPES
½ cup wholemeal plain flour
½ cup white plain flour
3 eggs, lightly beaten
1¼ cups milk
15g butter, melted
1 cup stale wholemeal breadcrumbs
¼ cup grated parmesan cheese
SPINACH AND RICOTTA FILLING
30g butter
1 clove garlic, crushed
1 bunch spinach (silverbeet),
    chopped
250g ricotta cheese
¼ cup grated parmesan cheese
¼ teaspoon ground cumin
SAUCE
30g butter
2 tablespoons wholemeal plain flour
1¼ cups skim milk

Crêpes: Sift flours into large bowl, make well in centre, gradually stir in combined eggs, milk and butter, mix to smooth batter (or blend or process all ingredients until smooth). Cover, stand for 30 minutes. Pour 2 to 3 tablespoons of batter into heated greased heavy-based crêpe pan, cook until lightly browned underneath. Turn crêpe, brown other side. Repeat with remaining batter. You will need 12 crêpes for this recipe.

Divide filling evenly between crêpes, roll up, place in single layer in lightly greased shallow ovenproof dish, top with sauce, sprinkle with combined breadcrumbs and cheese. Bake in moderate oven for about 30 minutes or until well browned.

Spinach and Ricotta Filling: Melt butter in medium frying pan, add garlic and spinach, stir over medium heat until spinach is tender and all liquid has evaporated. Process spinach with the remaining ingredients until finely chopped.

Sauce: Melt butter in small saucepan, stir in flour, stir over medium heat 1 minute (or microwave on HIGH for 1 minute). Remove from heat, gradually stir in milk, stir over high heat (or microwave on HIGH about 2 minutes) until mixture boils and thickens.

Serves 6.

RIGHT: From left: Whole-Wheat Swiss Chard and Ricotta Crepes; Vegetable and Tofu Lasagne.

VEGETABLE AND TOFU LASAGNE

Lasagne can be prepared a day ahead; keep, covered, in refrigerator. Lasagne can be frozen for a month. Cooked packaged lasagne can be used; you will need 150g (9 sheets) of wholemeal lasagne noodles.

1 tablespoon oil
2 medium onions, chopped
2 cloves garlic, crushed
2 medium carrots, chopped
2 large sticks celery, chopped
1 medium red pepper, chopped
200g mushrooms, chopped
6 medium tomatoes, peeled, chopped
2 tablespoons tomato paste
¼ cup chopped fresh basil
¼ cup chopped fresh parsley
¾ cup soft tofu
300g fresh wholemeal lasagne noodles
¼ cup stale wholemeal breadcrumbs
1 tablespoon grated parmesan cheese

Heat oil in large saucepan, add onions, garlic, carrots, celery and pepper, stir over medium heat for about 5 minutes (or microwave on HIGH for about 5 minutes) or until onions are soft. Add mushrooms, stir over medium heat for 1 minute (or microwave on HIGH for 1 minute). Stir in tomatoes, paste and herbs, bring to boil, reduce heat, cover, simmer for about 15 minutes (or microwave on HIGH for about 5 minutes) or until vegetables are tender. Remove from heat.

Beat tofu in small bowl until smooth, add ¼ cup of the tofu to vegetable mixture, mix well.

Cut pasta into 6 rectangles measuring about 10cm x 26cm. Spread a third of the vegetable mixture into greased 20cm x 26cm ovenproof dish (2 litre capacity). Top with 2 sheets of pasta. Continue layering vegetable mixture and pasta, finishing with a layer of pasta.

Spread remaining tofu evenly over pasta, sprinkle with combined breadcrumbs and cheese. Bake in moderate oven for about 50 minutes or until golden brown (or microwave on HIGH for about 25 minutes).

Serves 4.

CREPES WITH CREAMY BROCCOLI FILLING

Crêpes can be made a day ahead; keep, covered, in refrigerator, or freeze for up to 2 months. Filling unsuitable to freeze.

CREPES
⅓ **cup wholemeal plain flour**
2 **tablespoons white self-raising flour**
2 **eggs, lightly beaten**
⅔ **cup milk**
1 **tablespoon oil**
¼ **cup grated parmesan cheese**
CREAMY BROCCOLI FILLING
750g **broccoli, chopped**
30g **butter**
2 **green shallots, chopped**
1 **tablespoon wholemeal plain flour**
1 **large vegetable stock cube,**
   crumbled
½ **cup milk**
½ **cup cream**
pinch ground nutmeg
1 **tablespoon chopped fresh basil**

Crêpes: Sift flours into large bowl, make well in centre, gradually stir in combined eggs, milk and oil, mix to a smooth batter (or blend or process all ingredients until smooth). Cover, stand for 30 minutes. Pour 2 to 3 tablespoons of batter into heated greased heavy-based crêpe pan; cook until lightly browned underneath. Turn crêpe, brown on other side. Repeat with remaining batter. You will need 8 crêpes for this recipe.

Divide filling between crêpes, fold crêpes into triangles. Place crêpes into lightly greased ovenproof dish, sprinkle with cheese, bake in moderate oven for about 10 minutes or until heated through.

Creamy Broccoli Filling: Boil, steam or microwave broccoli until tender, drain. Melt butter in medium saucepan, add shallots, stir over medium heat for 1 minute (or microwave on HIGH for 1 minute). Stir in flour, stir over medium heat for 1 minute (or microwave on HIGH for 1 minute). Remove from heat, gradually stir in combined stock cube, milk, cream and nutmeg, stir over high heat (or microwave on HIGH for about 2 minutes) until mixture boils and thickens; stir in broccoli and basil.

Serves 4.

From left: Pea Soufflé Omelettes; Crêpes with Creamy Broccoli Filling.

Table and jug: Country Form

PEA SOUFFLE OMELETTES

Make omelettes just before serving. Sauce can be made a day ahead; keep, covered in refrigerator. Recipe unsuitable to freeze.

1 cup fresh or frozen peas
4 eggs, separated
¼ cup grated tasty cheese
VEGETABLE SAUCE
30g butter
1 small onion, thinly sliced
1 stick celery, thinly sliced
1 small carrot, thinly sliced
1 tablespoon wholemeal plain flour
1¼ cups water
2 tablespoons sour cream
1 tablespoon chopped fresh mint

Boil, steam or microwave peas until tender; drain. Blend or process peas until smooth; push through sieve.

Beat egg yolks in large bowl until thick, stir in pea puree. Beat egg whites in medium bowl until soft peaks form, gently fold into pea mixture. Pour half the mixture into heated greased small frying pan, cook over high heat until browned underneath, place pan under hot griller until surface of omelette is set.

Sprinkle omelette with cheese, fold in half, place on serving plate; serve immediately. Repeat with remaining mixture. Serve omelettes with vegetable sauce.

Vegetable Sauce: Melt butter in medium saucepan, add onion, celery and carrot, stir over medium heat for about 3 minutes (or microwave on HIGH for about 4 minutes) or until carrot is soft. Stir in flour, stir over medium heat for 1 minute (or microwave on HIGH for 1 minute). Remove from heat, gradually stir in water, stir over high heat until mixture boils and thickens slightly. Stir in sour cream and mint.

Serves 2.

SUMMER VEGETABLE FLAN

Flan can be made up to a day ahead; keep, covered, in refrigerator. Recipe unsuitable to freeze or microwave.

PASTRY
½ cup white plain flour
½ cup wholemeal plain flour
2 tablespoons oil
1 egg, lightly beaten
1 tablespoon water, approximately
FILLING
30g butter
4 green shallots, chopped
1 tablespoon chopped fresh basil
2 medium zucchini, sliced
10 lettuce leaves, sliced
3 eggs, lightly beaten
300g carton sour cream
½ cup grated tasty cheese

Pastry: Sift flours into medium bowl, Add combined oil and egg with enough water to mix to a firm dough. Knead gently on lightly floured surface until smooth, cover; refrigerate for 30 minutes. Roll pastry large enough to line 23cm flan tin, trim edge.

Cover pastry with greaseproof paper, fill with dried beans or rice. Bake in moderately hot oven for 15 minutes, remove paper and beans, bake further 10 minutes or until golden brown, cool.

Filling: Melt butter in medium saucepan, add shallots and basil, stir over medium heat for 1 minute. Add zucchini and lettuce, stir over medium heat for about 5 minutes or until vegetables are soft; cool. Combine eggs, cream and cheese in a medium bowl; mix well.

Spread lettuce mixture evenly over pastry. Gradually pour egg mixture over lettuce. Bake in moderate oven for about 30 minutes or until set, stand for 5 minutes before serving.

Summer Vegetable Flan.

Accompaniments

The good, healthy variety here includes mostly salads plus some new and different vegetable dishes. They can be served as entrées, as accompaniments to a main dish or as main courses, if you like. Many have tasty dressings which add a special zest.

HERBED RICE WITH SPINACH

Recipe is best prepared close to serving time. This recipe is unsuitable to freeze.

1 tablespoon oil
1 medium onion, chopped
1 clove garlic, crushed
1 cup long grain rice
1 large vegetable stock cube, crumbled
2 cups water
½ teaspoon ground turmeric
¼ teaspoon ground nutmeg
½ bunch (20 leaves) English spinach, chopped
2 tablespoons chopped fresh chives
1 tablespoon chopped fresh parsley

Heat oil in medium frying pan, add onion and garlic, stir over medium heat for about 2 minutes (or microwave on HIGH for about 3 minutes) or until onion is soft. Add rice, stir until rice is coated with oil, stir in stock cube, water, turmeric and nutmeg. Bring to boil, stir in spinach and herbs. Transfer mixture to large ovenproof dish (4 cup capacity), cover, bake in moderate oven for about 25 minutes (or microwave on HIGH for about 20 minutes) or until liquid is absorbed and rice is tender; stir rice before serving.
Serves 4.

COUSCOUS AND PICKLED GINGER SALAD

Prepare salad close to serving time. This recipe is not suitable to freeze or microwave.

1 cup couscous
50g packet red pickled ginger
1 medium apple
3 green shallots, chopped
HERB VINAIGRETTE
¼ cup oil
¼ cup cider vinegar
¼ teaspoon dried oregano leaves
1 tablespoon chopped fresh chives

Place couscous in large bowl, cover with boiling water, stand for 8 minutes. Drain in fine strainer, rinse under cold water. Turn couscous onto tray covered with absorbent paper, dry as much as possible. Rinse ginger, drain well. Peel apple and cut into thin strips. Combine couscous, ginger, apple and shallots in large bowl, add vinaigrette, toss gently.
Herb Vinaigrette: Combine all ingredients in jar, shake well.
Serves 6.

PEPPER SALAD WITH CRACKED WHEAT

Salad can be prepared several hours ahead; keep, covered, in refrigerator. Add dressing just before serving. Recipe unsuitable to freeze.

2 tablespoons sesame seeds
⅓ cup cracked wheat
2 medium carrots, chopped
2 sticks celery, chopped
1 medium tomato, chopped
1 medium green pepper, chopped
1 medium red pepper, chopped
1 small cucumber, chopped
DRESSING
2 tablespoons olive oil
2 tablespoons lemon juice
1 clove garlic, crushed
1 tablespoon chopped fresh basil

Stir seeds over medium heat in small heavy-based frying pan until lightly browned. Remove from pan, cool.

Place wheat in small bowl, cover with boiling water, stand for 15 minutes. Drain in fine strainer, rinse well under cold water. Turn wheat onto tray covered with absorbent paper. Dry as much as possible. Combine wheat with remaining ingredients in large bowl, pour over dressing, toss gently.
Dressing: Combine all ingredients in jar, shake well.
Serves 4.

FENNEL WITH ORANGE SAUCE

Recipe can be made several hours ahead; keep, covered, in refrigerator. Reheat before serving. Recipe unsuitable to freeze.

2 medium oranges
¼ cup slivered almonds
1 tablespoon oil
1 clove garlic, crushed
2 medium fennel bulbs, sliced
½ teaspoon cornflour

Grate enough rind from 1 orange to give 2 teaspoons rind. Peel some skin thinly from the remaining orange, cut into thin strips. You need about 1 tablespoon strips.

Drop strips into small saucepan of boiling water, drain immediately. Squeeze enough juice from oranges to give ½ cup juice.

Toast nuts on oven tray in moderate oven for about 5 minutes, cool.

Heat oil in medium frying pan, add garlic and fennel, stir over medium heat for about 5 minutes (or microwave on HIGH for about 3 minutes) or until fennel is tender; keep warm. Add grated rind and cornflour blended with orange juice to pan, stir over high heat (or microwave on HIGH) until mixture boils and thickens slightly. Pour sauce over fennel, add nuts and orange strips before serving.
Serves 4.

Clockwise from left: Herbed Rice with Spinach; Couscous and Pickled Ginger Salad; Pepper Salad with Cracked Wheat.

Wooden bowls: Corso de Fiori; cream bowl: Country Form; chair: John Normyle (left)

SPINACH AND YOGHURT POTATO SKINS

Spinach mixture can be made a day ahead; keep, covered, in refrigerator. Potato skins can be cooked several hours ahead; top with spinach mixture just before baking. We used Pontiac potatoes in this recipe. Recipe unsuitable to freeze or microwave.

4 large potatoes
1 tablespoon oil
2 teaspoons oil, extra
1 clove garlic, crushed
250g packet frozen spinach, thawed
2 tablespoons plain yoghurt
1 cup stale wholemeal breadcrumbs
15g butter, melted

Place potatoes on oven tray, bake in moderate oven for about 1¼ hours or until tender. Cut potatoes into quarters, scoop out the flesh leaving a 5mm shell of potato; reserve flesh. Brush potato skins inside and out with oil, place onto oven tray, cut side up; bake in hot oven for 10 minutes. Chop reserved potato flesh.

Heat extra oil in medium frying pan, add garlic and drained spinach, stir over heat about 3 minutes or until liquid has evaporated. Remove from heat, stir in potato flesh, yoghurt and half the breadcrumbs; cool slightly. Combine remaining breadcrumbs and

SUMMER SALAD WITH YOGHURT CHIVE DRESSING

Salad can be prepared several hours ahead; keep, covered, in refrigerator. Recipe unsuitable to freeze.

⅓ **bunch curly endive, chopped**
1 **small cucumber, chopped**
1 **cup watercress sprigs**
8 **cherry tomatoes, halved**
1 **medium turnip, chopped**
1 **medium avocado, sliced**
YOGHURT CHIVE DRESSING
¾ **cup plain yoghurt**
1 **tablespoon lemon juice**
¼ **cup chopped fresh chives**

Combine endive, cucumber, watercress, tomatoes and turnip in large bowl, add avocado and dressing; toss gently to combine.
Yoghurt Chive Dressing: Combine all ingredients in small bowl.
Serves 4.

BELOW: Summer Salad with Yoghurt Chive Dressing.

Bowl: Corso de Fiori (below)

butter in small bowl. Spoon spinach mixture onto potato skins, sprinkle with breadcrumb mixture, bake in moderately hot oven for about 10 minutes or until breadcrumbs are lightly browned.
Serves 4 to 6.

ABOVE: From left: Spinach and Yoghurt Potato Skins; Fennel with Orange Sauce.

Terracotta dish: Mosmania (above)

FRUIT AND RICE SALAD

Salad can be made several hours ahead; keep, covered, in refrigerator. Recipe unsuitable to freeze.

¼ cup pine nuts
1 cup brown rice
2 tablespoons lemon juice
2 tablespoons oil
1 tablespoon chutney
2 teaspoons curry powder
1 small carrot, chopped
1 medium apple, chopped
1½ cups chopped pineapple
1 small red pepper, chopped
¼ cup chopped raisins
¼ cup chopped walnuts

Toast pine nuts on oven tray in moderate oven for about 5 minutes, cool. Add rice gradually to large saucepan of boiling water, boil, uncovered, for 30 minutes or until rice is tender, drain, rinse under cold water; drain. Combine rice, juice, oil, chutney, curry powder, carrot, apple, pineapple, pepper, raisins and nuts in large bowl; mix well.
Serves 6.

WITLOF AND FRUIT SALAD

Salad can be prepared several hours ahead; keep, covered, in refrigerator. Add dressing just before serving. Recipe unsuitable to freeze.

4 witlof, chopped
3 sticks celery, sliced
1 cup watercress sprigs
3 medium oranges
ORANGE DRESSING
⅓ cup olive oil
¼ cup orange juice
¼ teaspoon prepared mustard
1 tablespoon chopped fresh parsley

Arrange witlof on serving plate. Combine celery, watercress and orange segments in medium bowl, serve over witlof. Top with dressing.
Orange Dressing: Combine all ingredients in jar, shake well.
Serves 4.

From left: Fruit and Rice Salad; Witlof and Fruit Salad

Salad bowl: Villa Italiana; salad servers: Made Where; wooden tray: Country Furniture Antiques (right).

BROCCOLI SALAD WITH GARLIC VINAIGRETTE

Salad can be made several hours ahead; keep, covered, in refrigerator. Add. dressing just before serving. Recipe unsuitable to freeze.

500g broccoli, chopped
½ x 250g punnet cherry tomatoes, halved
2 cups (120g) bean sprouts
1 cup sultanas
GARLIC VINAIGRETTE
½ cup olive oil
2 tablespoons lemon juice
1 clove garlic, crushed
Boil, steam or microwave broccoli until just tender, drain, rinse under cold water, drain. Combine broccoli, tomatoes, sprouts and sultanas in large bowl, add dressing; toss gently.
Garlic Vinaigrette: Combine all ingredients in jar; shake well.
Serves 4.

HOT SPINACH AND PEA SALAD

Salad is best made just before serving. Recipe unsuitable to freeze.

1 tablespoon sesame seeds
¼ cup oil
1 clove garlic, crushed
250g small mushrooms, sliced
4 medium spinach (silverbeet) leaves, shredded
1 cup frozen peas, thawed
2 cups (120g) bean sprouts
2 teaspoons light soy sauce
1 tablespoon lemon juice
1 teaspoon grated fresh ginger
Stir sesame seeds over heat in heavy-based frying pan until lightly browned, remove from pan, cool.

Heat a tablespoon of the oil in large frying pan, add garlic, mushrooms and spinach, stir over medium heat for about 2 minutes (or microwave on HIGH for about 2 minutes) or until mushrooms are soft. Add peas and bean sprouts, stir over medium heat for 3 minutes (or microwave on HIGH for 2 minutes). Add combined remaining oil, sauce, juice and ginger, stir over medium heat for 1 minute (or microwave on HIGH for 1 minute). Sprinkle salad with sesame seeds just before serving.
Serves 4.

ASPARAGUS ZUCCHINI STIR-FRY

Recipe is best cooked close to serving time. Recipe unsuitable to freeze.

1 bunch fresh asparagus
4 medium zucchini
30g butter
2 tablespoons pine nuts
2 tablespoons chopped fresh chives
Cut asparagus into 5cm lengths. Cut zucchini into thick strips about 5cm in length. Melt butter in medium frying pan, add asparagus, zucchini and pine nuts, stir over medium heat (or microwave on HIGH for about 4 minutes) until asparagus is tender and nuts are browned. Stir in chives.
Serves 4.

BROAD BEAN AND ZUCCHINI SALAD

Salad can be made a day ahead; keep, covered, in refrigerator. Recipe unsuitable to freeze.

250g fresh or frozen broad beans
4 medium zucchini, sliced
1 medium red pepper, chopped
1 medium onion, sliced
½ cup black olives
200g feta cheese, chopped
DRESSING
¼ cup olive oil
¼ cup lemon juice
1 clove garlic, crushed

Boil, steam or microwave beans until tender, drain; rinse under cold water, drain. Boil, steam or microwave zucchini until just tender, drain; rinse under cold water, drain.

Combine beans, zucchini, pepper, onion, olives and cheese in large bowl, add dressing, toss gently.

Dressing: Combine all ingredients in jar, shake well.

CURRIED APPLE AND CELERY SALAD

Prepare salad close to serving time. This recipe is not suitable to freeze or microwave.

¾ cup slivered almonds
4 sticks celery, chopped
2 medium apples, chopped
¾ cup raisins
1 tablespoon chopped fresh parsley
CURRY DRESSING
⅓ cup sour cream
2 tablespoons mayonnaise
1 teaspoon curry powder
2 tablespoons orange juice

Toast almonds on oven tray in moderate oven for about 5 minutes, cool. Combine celery, apples, raisins, almonds and parsley in large bowl; add dressing, mix well.

Curry Dressing: Combine all ingredients in small bowl, mix well.

Serves 4.

CRUNCHY RED CABBAGE SALAD

Salad can be made a day ahead; keep, covered, in refrigerator. Recipe unsuitable to freeze.

¾ cup blanched almonds
¼ cup water
1 teaspoon caraway seeds
1 tablespoon tamari shoyu
12 green shallots, chopped
1 small red cabbage, shredded
3 sticks celery, chopped
1 mignonette lettuce

Blend or process almonds, water, seeds and tamari shoyu until smooth. Combine with shallots, cabbage and celery in large bowl; mix well. Serve over lettuce leaves.

Serves 4.

BELOW: Asparagus Zucchini Stir-Fry.
LEFT: From top: Hot Spinach and Pea Salad; Broccoli Salad with Garlic Vinaigrette.

Bowls and basket: Corso de Fiori; box: Country Form; table: John Normyle (left); plate and bowl: Mikasa; spoon and fork: Made Where (below)

Clockwise from left: Broad Bean and Zucchini Salad;
Crunchy Red Cabbage Salad; Curried Apple and Celery Salad.

Plates: Mikasa; spoon: Made Where; table: The Country Trader (above)

HERBED MUSHROOM SALAD

Salad can be made a day ahead; keep, covered, in refrigerator. Recipe unsuitable to freeze.

375g baby mushrooms, sliced
3 green shallots, chopped
1 medium carrot, grated
2 tablespoons chopped fresh parsley
1 tablespoon chopped fresh chives
1 cup bean sprouts
DRESSING
⅓ cup olive oil
¼ cup lemon juice
2 tablespoons cider vinegar
½ teaspoon raw sugar
Combine mushrooms, shallots, carrot, parsley, chives and sprouts in medium bowl, add dressing; stir well.
Dressing: Combine all ingredients in jar, shake well.
Serves 4.

SQUASH WITH BASIL AND HONEY

Recipe is best made just before serving. Recipe unsuitable to freeze.

1 tablespoon sesame seeds
12 yellow squash
2 teaspoons olive oil
1 small onion, finely chopped
1 clove garlic, crushed
1 tablespoon honey
1 teaspoon light soy sauce
1 tablespoon tahini
⅓ cup chopped fresh basil

Stir seeds over medium heat in small heavy-based frying pan until lightly browned. Remove from pan, cool.

Boil, steam or microwave squash until tender; drain, cool. Trim slices from bases so they sit flat; scoop a shallow round from top of each squash. Chop trimmed pieces finely.

Heat oil in small saucepan, add onion and garlic, stir over medium heat for about 2 minutes (or microwave on HIGH for about 2 minutes) or until onion is soft. Add chopped squash, honey, sauce, tahini and basil, cook over medium heat for 1 minute (or microwave on HIGH for 1 minute).

Place squash onto oven tray, spoon basil mixture into hollows, sprinkle with seeds, bake in moderate oven for about 10 minutes (or microwave on HIGH for about 3 minutes) or until heated through.
Serves 4.

CAULIFLOWER IN HERBED TOMATO SAUCE

Recipe can be prepared several hours ahead; keep, covered, in refrigerator. Recipe unsuitable to freeze or microwave.

1 tablespoon oil
1 clove garlic, crushed
1 medium onion, chopped
2 sticks celery, sliced
½ medium cauliflower, chopped
425g can tomatoes
415ml can tomato purée
½ large vegetable stock cube, crumbled
½ cup water
1 tablespoon chopped fresh oregano
1 tablespoon chopped fresh basil
1 teaspoon raw sugar
¼ cup grated fresh parmesan cheese
Heat oil in large frying pan, add garlic, onion and celery, stir over heat until onion is soft. Add cauliflower, undrained crushed tomatoes, purée, stock cube, water, oregano, basil and sugar. Bring to boil, reduce heat, simmer, uncovered, for about 30 minutes or until mixture is thick and cauliflower is tender. Serve topped with cheese.
Serves 6.

BELOW: Squash with Basil and Honey.
LEFT. Herbed Mushroom Salad.

Setting: Made Where (below)

POTATO SALAD WITH CIDER VINEGAR DRESSING

Salad can be made several hours ahead; keep, covered, in refrigerator. Recipe unsuitable to freeze.

¼ cup slivered almonds
5 medium potatoes
3 sticks celery, chopped
4 green shallots, chopped
1 medium apple, chopped
1 tablespoon lemon juice
CIDER VINEGAR DRESSING
2 tablespoons cider vinegar
⅓ cup olive oil
2 teaspoons lemon juice
2 teaspoons brown sugar
¼ teaspoon dry mustard
1 clove garlic, crushed

Toast almonds on oven tray in moderate oven for 5 minutes: cool.

Boil, steam or microwave potatoes until just tender; cool. Peel potatoes, cut into cubes. Combine potatoes with remaining ingredients in large bowl. Add dressing, toss gently.

Cider Vinegar Dressing: Combine all ingredients in jar, shake well.

Serves 4.

SNOW PEA, APPLE AND NUT SALAD

Prepare salad close to serving time. Recipe unsuitable to freeze.

500g snow peas
1 medium apple, sliced
1 tablespoon lemon juice
1 cup pecan nuts or walnuts
CHIVE DRESSING
¼ cup mayonnaise
½ cup plain yoghurt
2 tablespoons chopped fresh chives

Boil, steam or microwave snow peas until just tender, drain; place in bowl of iced water, drain. Toss apple in juice. Combine all ingredients in a large bowl, add dressing; toss gently.

Chive Dressing: Combine all ingredients in medium bowl; mix well.

Serves 4.

MINTED PARSLEY SALAD

Salad can be prepared a day ahead; keep, covered, in refrigerator. Recipe unsuitable to freeze or microwave.

½ cup cracked wheat
2 cups chopped fresh parsley
4 green shallots, chopped
250g punnet cherry tomatoes, halved
1 small cucumber, chopped
1 stick celery, chopped
⅓ cup chopped fresh mint
⅓ cup lemon juice
1 tablespoon oil

Place wheat in small bowl, cover with boiling water, stand for 15 minutes. Drain in fine strainer, rinse well under cold water. Turn wheat onto tray covered with absorbent paper, dry as much as possible. Combine all ingredients in large bowl, mix well.

Serves 4.

BELOW: Cauliflower in Herbed Tomato Sauce. RIGHT: Clockwise from left: Potato Salad with Cider Vinegar Dressing; Minted Parsley Salad; Snow Pea, Apple and Nut Salad.

Salad bowls and nutcracker: Shop 3, Balmain (right); plate: Villa Italiania; chair: Corso de Fiori (below)

Desserts

A feature of our desserts is that most are based on fruit with all its luscious flavour and goodness. You have the choice of rich or not-so-rich; hot, cold or frozen (and note the quick-mix pudding to make for Christmas or for a wonderful winter treat). They'd be great as party makers or the perfect finish to a meal.

STRAWBERRY AND LIME SORBET

Sorbet can be made 3 days ahead.

2 punnets (500g) strawberries
1 teaspoon grated lime rind
¼ cup lime juice
⅔ cup sifted icing sugar
2 egg whites

Blend or process strawberries, rind, juice, sugar and egg whites until smooth, creamy and pale in colour. Pour mixture into lamington pan. Cover with foil, freeze overnight.
    Serves 6.

BELOW: Strawberry and Lime Sorbet.
RIGHT: Clockwise from left: Chestnut Carob Mousse; Apple Polenta Flan; Baked Peach Cheesecake.

Glass: Studio-Haus (below)

CHESTNUT CAROB MOUSSE

Mousse can be made 2 days ahead; keep, covered, in refrigerator. Recipe unsuitable to freeze.

225g milk carob, melted
1 egg, separated
250g can chestnut spread
300ml carton cream

Place carob in medium bowl, cool; do not allow to set. Gradually stir in combined egg yolk and chestnut spread. Beat cream in small bowl until soft peaks form, fold into carob mixture. Beat egg white in small bowl until soft peaks form, fold into carob mixture. Pour into 8 serving glasses; refrigerate until set. Serve with extra whipped cream, if desired.
Serves 8.

BAKED PEACH CHEESECAKE

Cheesecake can be made a day ahead; keep, covered, in refrigerator. Recipe unsuitable to freeze or microwave.

185g butter, melted
3 cups (375g) plain sweet biscuit crumbs
3 medium fresh peaches, sliced
¼ teaspoon ground nutmeg
CHEESE FILLING
200g ricotta cheese
½ cup brown sugar
½ cup sour cream
3 eggs, separated
1 tablespoon white plain flour
1 tablespoon lemon juice

Combine butter and crumbs in large bowl, mix well. Press evenly over base and side of 20cm springform tin, refrigerate for 30 minutes. Arrange peach slices over base, sprinkle with nutmeg, pour cheese filling over peaches. Bake in moderately slow oven for about 1 hour or until set. Cool in oven with door ajar; refrigerate several hours before serving.
Cheese Filling: Beat cheese, sugar, cream, egg yolks, flour and juice in a medium bowl with electric mixer until smooth. Beat egg whites in a medium bowl until soft peaks form, fold lightly into cheese mixture.

APPLE POLENTA FLAN

Flan can be made a day ahead; keep, covered, in refrigerator. Recipe unsuitable to freeze or microwave.

1 litre (4 cups) milk
¾ cup castor sugar
45g butter
3 teaspoons grated lemon rind
1 cup polenta
¾ cup sultanas
⅓ cup chopped walnuts
½ cup cream
1 large apple, thinly sliced
1½ tablespoons maple syrup
3 teaspoons castor sugar, extra
½ teaspoon ground cinnamon

Grease 20cm springform tin. Heat milk, sugar, butter and rind in medium saucepan, stir over high heat, without boiling, until sugar is dissolved. Bring to boil, reduce heat, stir in polenta, cover, cook over low heat for 10 minutes, stirring occasionally. Remove from heat, stir in sultanas, walnuts and cream. Pour into prepared tin, top with apple. Pour syrup over apple. Sprinkle with combined extra sugar and cinnamon. Bake in moderate oven for about 35 minutes or until apple is tender and flan has come slightly away from side of tin; cool to room temperature. Remove from tin, serve with extra maple syrup if desired.

SUNFLOWER FRUIT SALAD

Fruit salad can be prepared a day ahead; keep, covered, in refrigerator. Add nuts and kernels just before serving. Recipe unsuitable to freeze.

250g punnet strawberries, halved
125g blueberries
1 medium kiwi fruit, sliced
½ medium rockmelon, chopped
½ cup orange juice
¼ cup slivered almonds
⅓ cup chopped pecan nuts
2 tablespoons sunflower seed kernels

Combine strawberries, blueberries, kiwi fruit, rockmelon, juice, nuts and kernels in large bowl, mix gently.
Serves 4.

BROWN SUGAR MERINGUES WITH CAROB CREAM

Meringues are best filled just before serving. Unfilled meringues can be made up to 3 days ahead; keep in an airtight container. Recipe unsuitable to freeze or microwave.

2 egg whites
½ cup brown sugar
CAROB CREAM
¼ cup cottage cheese
1 tablespoon plain yogurt
40g milk carob, grated
2 teaspoons honey

Lightly grease 2 oven trays, cover with greaseproof paper. Beat egg whites in small bowl until soft peaks form. Add sugar gradually; beat until dissolved between each addition. Spoon mixture into large piping bag fitted with 1cm plain tube. Pipe swirls of mixture, about 6cm long, onto prepared trays. Bake in very slow oven for about 2 hours or until firm to touch; cool on trays. join with carob cream.
Carob Cream: Press cottage cheese through fine sieve into small bowl, stir in yoghurt, carob and honey.
Makes about 12.

From top: Sunflower Fruit Salad; Brown Sugar Meringues with Carob Cream.

Marble slab: Appley Hoare Antiques

QUICK-MIX CHRISTMAS PUDDING

You will need to cook about 350g pumpkin for this recipe. Pudding can be made a week ahead; keep, covered, in refrigerator. Pudding can also be frozen for up to 2 months. Recipe unsuitable to microwave.

1½ cups wholemeal self-raising flour
1 teaspoon mixed spice
1 teaspoon ground ginger
1 cup stale wholemeal breadcrumbs
1 cup chopped dates
½ cup chopped raisins
½ cup chopped dried apricots
60g butter
⅓ cup honey
1 cup cold mashed pumpkin
2 eggs, lightly beaten

Sift flour and spices into large bowl, stir in breadcrumbs and fruit. Combine butter and honey in small saucepan, stir over low heat (or microwave on HIGH for about 1 minute) until butter is melted. Stir honey mixture into bowl with pumpkin and eggs.

Spoon mixture into well-greased steamer (7 cup capacity), cover tightly. Place pudding in large boiler with enough boiling water to come halfway up side of steamer. Cover tightly, boil for 2 hours, adding more boiling water as it evaporates during cooking time. Serve with yoghurt sprinkled with nutmeg, if desired.

PEARS WITH APRICOT FRUIT SAUCE

Pears are best cooked just before serving. Sauce can be made several hours ahead; keep, covered, in refrigerator. Recipe unsuitable to freeze or microwave.

6 medium pears
3 cups water
½ cup lemon juice
½ cup raw sugar
1 cinnamon stick
2 teaspoons grated fresh ginger
APRICOT FRUIT SAUCE
1¼ cups apricot nectar
¾ cup water
¼ cup raw sugar
¾ cup (110g) dried apricots
2 teaspoons cornflour
1 tablespoon water, extra
½ x 250g punnet strawberries, sliced
125g blueberries
1 medium kiwi fruit, sliced

Peel pears, leave stems intact. Combine water, juice, sugar, cinnamon stick and ginger in large saucepan, stir over high heat, without boiling, until sugar is dissolved. Bring to boil, reduce heat, stand pears in pan, cover, simmer for about 20 minutes or until pears are tender. Serve warm with apricot fruit sauce.

Apricot Fruit Sauce: Combine nectar, water and sugar in large saucepan, stir over high heat, without boiling, until sugar is dissolved. Bring to boil, reduce heat, add apricots, simmer for 5 minutes. Blend cornflour with extra water, stir into mixture, stir over high heat until mixture boils and thickens. Add berries and kiwi fruit.

Serves 6.

FROZEN COCONUT CREAM AND MANGO CAKE

Cake can be made a week ahead: keep covered in freezer.

400ml can coconut cream
½ cup plain yoghurt
2 tablespoons honey
MANGO SORBET
2 medium mangoes
2 teaspoons grated orange rind
½ cup orange juice
2 tablespoons honey
2 egg whites

Line base and side of 20cm springform tin with plastic wrap.

Combine coconut cream, yoghurt and honey in medium bowl. Pour mixture into loaf pan, cover with foil, freeze until partly frozen.

Place mixture into medium bowl, beat with electric mixer until smooth. Spoon evenly into prepared springform tin, cover, freeze for 1 hour or until firm. Top with mango sorbet, cover, freeze for several hours or until set. Serve with extra mango, if desired.

Mango Sorbet: Blend or process mangoes until smooth; you need 2 cups purée for this recipe. Combine mango, rind, juice and honey in medium bowl. Pour mixture into loaf pan, cover with foil and freeze until partly frozen.

Place mixture into medium bowl, beat with electric mixer until smooth. Beat egg whites in small bowl until soft peaks form, fold into mango mixture.

LEFT: Quick-Mix Christmas Pudding.
ABOVE: Frozen Coconut Cream and
Mango Cake. ABOVE LEFT: Pears with
Apricot Fruit Sauce.

Plate: The Bay Tree (left); plate: Shop 3, Balmain; rug: Mosmania (above); plates and place mats: Made Where (above left)

BUCKWHEAT BANANA PANCAKES

Make pancakes close to serving time. Sauce can be made a day ahead; keep, covered, in refrigerator. This recipe is not suitable to freeze or microwave.

PANCAKES
¼ cup buckwheat flour
1 medium banana
2 eggs
¾ cup milk
1 tablespoon lemon juice
ORANGE SAUCE
30g butter
¼ cup sugar
1 cup orange juice
1 tablespoon cornflour
1 tablespoon water

Pancakes: Blend or process all ingredients until smooth. Transfer batter to medium jug; cover, stand for 30 minutes. Pour 2 to 3 tablespoons of batter into heated greased heavy-based small frying pan, cook until lightly browned underneath. Turn pancake, brown on other side. Repeat with remaining batter. You will need 8 pancakes for this recipe. Fold pancakes as desired. Serve with orange sauce.

Orange Sauce: Melt butter in a medium saucepan, add sugar, stir over low heat for about 3 minutes or until sugar is dissolved and mixture is golden brown. Add juice, stir over heat, without boiling, until mixture is smooth. Blend cornflour with water, stir into orange mixture. Stir over heat until sauce boils and thickens.

Serves 4.

HONEYED MUESLI AND RICOTTA FLAN

Flan can be made 3 days ahead; keep, covered, in refrigerator. Recipe unsuitable to freeze or microwave.

1 cup untoasted muesli
30g butter, melted
3 teaspoons honey
300g ricotta cheese
1½ tablespoons honey, extra
1 teaspoon grated lemon rind
⅓ cup plain yoghurt
1 egg, lightly beaten
¼ cup chopped dried apricots

Lightly grease shallow 20cm flan tin. Process muesli, butter and honey until roughly chopped. Press mixture firmly over base of prepared tin, refrigerate until firm.

Combine cheese, extra honey and rind in medium bowl, beat with electric mixer until smooth. Stir in yoghurt, egg and apricots. Spread mixture evenly over prepared base. Bake in moderately slow oven for about 30 minutes or until firm; cool. Refrigerate for several hours before serving. Decorate with whipped cream and lemon rind shreds, if desired.

BELOW: Peach and Sour Cream Flans.
LEFT: From top: Honeyed Muesli and Ricotta Flan; Buckwheat Banana Pancakes.

Plate: Studio-Haus (below); glass cake stand and table: The Country Trader; plate: Studio-Haus (left)

PEACH AND SOUR CREAM FLANS

Flans can be made a day ahead; keep, covered, in refrigerator. Recipe unsuitable to freeze or microwave.

PASTRY
¼ cup white self-raising flour
¾ cup white plain flour
1 cup wholemeal plain flour
155g butter
2 tablespoons water, approximately
6 medium peaches, sliced
FILLING
300g carton sour cream
1 egg, lightly beaten
⅓ cup sugar
1½ tablespoons white plain flour
2 teaspoons lemon juice

Pastry: Sift flours into large bowl, rub in butter. Add enough water to mix to a firm dough. Cover with plastic wrap, refrigerate for 30 minutes. Divide pastry evenly into 8 portions. Roll out each portion on lightly floured surface until large enough to line 8 x 9cm flan tins. Place on oven trays.

Cover pastry cases with greaseproof paper, fill with dried beans or rice. Bake in moderately hot oven for 7 minutes. Remove paper and beans, bake further 7 minutes, cool slightly. Place peaches into pastry cases, top with filling. Bake in moderate oven for 35 minutes or until filling is set. Serve hot or cold.

Filling: Combine all ingredients in a medium bowl, mix well.

Makes 8.

APRICOT AND PEAR WHIP

Dessert can be made 3 hours ahead; keep, covered, in refrigerator. Recipe unsuitable to freeze or microwave.

3 medium pears, chopped
1 cup dried apricots
¾ cup water
1 tablespoon sugar
⅓ cup plain yoghurt
2 egg whites

Combine pears, apricots and water in medium saucepan. Bring to boil, then reduce heat, cover, simmer for about 15 minutes or until apricots are soft, add sugar; cool to room temperature. Blend or process apricot mixture until it becomes smooth, add yoghurt, blend until combined. Transfer mixture to large bowl.

Beat egg whites in small bowl until soft peaks form, fold lightly into apricot mixture in 2 batches. Pour mixture into 6 serving dishes, and refrigerate well before serving.

Serves 6.

MAPLE AND BANANA FROZEN YOGHURT

Dessert can be made 3 days ahead; remove from freezer 15 minutes before serving. You will need about 3 medium bananas for this recipe.

1 cup mashed banana
¼ cup lemon juice
⅓ cup maple syrup
500g carton plain yoghurt
½ teaspoon ground nutmeg
1 egg white

Blend or process banana, juice, syrup, yoghurt and nutmeg until smooth. Pour mixture into freezer tray or deep cake pan, cover with foil, freeze until firm. Chop frozen mixture roughly, beat in small bowl with electric mixer until slightly softened. Add egg white, beat until mixture is smooth. Return mixture to freezer tray, cover, freeze until firm.

Serves 6.

FRESH FIGS WITH YOGHURT AND COCONUT

Recipe unsuitable to freeze.

1 cup flaked coconut
8 fresh figs
200g carton plain yoghurt
1 teaspoon grated lemon rind
2 tablespoons golden syrup

Stir coconut over low heat in heavy-based frying pan until lightly browned. Remove from pan to cool.

Remove stems from figs, cut into quarters. Divide figs between 4 dishes. Combine yoghurt, rind and golden syrup in small bowl; mix well. Pour yoghurt mixture over figs and sprinkle with coconut.

Serves 4.

Clockwise from left: Apricot and Pear Whip; Maple and Banana Frozen Yoghurt; Fresh Figs with Yoghurt and Coconut.

Plate: Studio-Haus

Healthy Drinks

Let's drink to fruit! There's no limit to the fruit you can put together in tangy, tantalising drinks; just choose lovely glasses to suit the occasion. They're great for children, too, as is our luscious sweet shake

BERRY LIME COCKTAIL

You will need about 12 medium limes for this recipe.

250g punnet strawberries, chopped
200g punnet raspberries
1 cup lime juice
1 cup unsweetened pineapple juice
1 tablespoon brown sugar
crushed ice
Blend or process all ingredients until smooth; strain before serving.
   Makes 1 litre (4 cups)

CAROB YOGHURT SHAKE

⅓ cup plain yoghurt
⅔ cup soy milk
1 teaspoon brown sugar
75g milk carob, melted
Blend all ingredients until they are thick and creamy.
   Makes 1½ cups.

Clockwise from left: Carob Yoghurt Shake; Berry Lime Cocktail; Apple Blackcurrant Zinger.

APPLE BLACKCURRANT ZINGER

Drink is best made just before serving; mixture will separate on standing.

100g fresh or frozen blackcurrants
3 cups apple juice
1 medium banana
Blend all ingredients until smooth.
   Makes 1 litre (4 cups).

From left: Mango Passionfruit Smoothie; Carrot, Apple and Celery Juice.

CARROT, APPLE AND CELERY JUICE

6 sticks celery
4 medium carrots
5 medium apples
2 teaspoons honey

Use juice extractor to make juice from celery, carrots and apples, following manufacturer's instructions. Combine juices in large jug, stir in honey. Refrigerate before serving.

Makes about 4 cups (1 litre).

MANGO PASSIONFRUIT SMOOTHIE

1 medium ripe mango, peeled, chopped
1 cup soy milk
1 tablespoon honey
1 passionfruit

Blend mango, milk and honey until smooth, stir in passionfruit. Refrigerate before serving.

Makes about 2 cups.

Baking and more

A fabulous feast awaits you in this section. There is a special-occasion torte and rich fruit cake among the cakes, plus scones, muffins, loaves, two particularly good teacakes, biscuits and more. Many are packed with fruit; others use vegetables deliciously. Many are simple; some are as rich as you could want.

BELOW: Carob Orange Torte.

CAROB ORANGE TORTE

Torte can be made 2 days ahead; keep, covered, in the refrigerator. Recipe unsuitable to freeze or microwave.

½ cup oil
1 teaspoon grated orange rind
½ cup orange juice
2 eggs, separated
1 tablespoon powdered coffee
   substitute
¼ cup brown sugar
¾ cup white self-raising flour
¾ cup wholemeal self-raising flour
1 tablespoon carob powder
1 teaspoon ground cinnamon
⅓ cup coconut
CREAM CHEESE FILLING
250g packet cream cheese
¼ cup sour cream
75g milk carob, melted
1 teaspoon brown sugar
½ teaspoon grated orange rind
TOPPING
40g milk carob, chopped
15g butter

Lightly grease deep 23cm round cake pan, line base with paper, grease paper. Combine oil, rind, juice, egg yolks, coffee substitute and sugar in large bowl; mix well. Stir in sifted flours, carob and cinnamon in 2 batches. Beat egg whites in small bowl until soft peaks form, fold into cake mixture in 2 batches. Spread mixture into prepared pan. Bake in moderate oven for about 40 minutes or until firm. Stand for 5 minutes before turning onto wire rack to cool.

Reserve ⅔ cup cream cheese filling. Split cake into 3 layers, sandwich layers with remaining filling. Spread and decorate cake with reserved filling. Press coconut onto side of cake.

Pour topping onto cake, tilt cake until topping covers surface evenly. When topping is starting to set, mark surface into desired number of servings. Refrigerate until firm. Decorate with strawberries, if desired.

Cream Cheese Filling: Beat cream cheese and sour cream in small bowl with electric mixer until smooth; beat in carob, sugar and rind.

Topping: Melt carob and butter in small bowl.

APRICOT SPIRAL TEACAKE

Teacake is best made on day of serving or can be frozen for 2 months. Recipe unsuitable to microwave.

2 cups white plain flour
20g compressed yeast
1 cup warm apple juice
2 cups wholemeal plain flour
2 teaspoons grated lemon rind
⅓ cup castor sugar
¼ cup oil
⅓ cup apple juice, extra
¼ cup honey
APRICOT FILLING
1½ cups (200g) dried apricots
2 teaspoons grated orange rind
½ cup orange juice
½ teaspoon ground cardamom
1 teaspoon vanilla essence
½ cup water
½ cup water, extra
HONEY PECAN TOPPING
1 cup rolled oats
1 cup pecan nuts
¼ cup oil
¼ cup honey
1 teaspoon ground cinnamon

Grease 2 deep 23cm round cake pans. Sift white flour into medium bowl, make well in centre. Gradually stir in crumbled yeast and juice; stir until smooth. Cover, stand in warm place for about 15 minutes, or until mixture rises slightly.

Sift wholemeal flour into large bowl, stir in rind, sugar and oil. Stir in yeast mixture and extra apple juice, mix to a soft dough. Turn dough onto lightly floured surface, knead for about 5 minutes or until dough is smooth and elastic. Place dough into lightly oiled bowl, cover, stand in warm place for about 1 hour or until dough has doubled in size.

Turn dough onto lightly floured surface, knead until smooth. Divide dough in half, roll 1 half to 25cm × 35cm rectangle. Spread half the filling evenly over dough. Sprinkle half the topping over filling.

Starting from long end, roll dough up like a Swiss roll. Pinch dough together at both ends. Place into a prepared pan, joining ends together. Using scissors, snip around top of dough at 3cm intervals. Cover, stand in warm place for about 1 hour or until dough has doubled in size.

Repeat with remaining dough, filling and topping. Bake teacakes in moderate oven for about 40 minutes. Turn onto wire rack, brush with warmed honey.

Apricot Filling: Combine apricots, rind, juice, cardamom, essence and water in medium saucepan, bring to boil, simmer, uncovered, for 15 minutes. Blend or process apricot mixture with extra water until smooth.

Honey Pecan Topping: Blend or process all ingredients until combined.

Makes 2.

CARAMEL TEACAKE ROLL

Teacake can be made a day ahead; keep in airtight container. Teacake can be frozen for 2 months. Recipe unsuitable to microwave.

7g sachet dry yeast
1 tablespoon honey
1 cup warm milk
1⅓ cups wholemeal plain flour
1½ cups white plain flour
¼ cup currants
1 egg, lightly beaten
45g butter, melted
icing sugar
CARAMEL FILLING
1 cup brown sugar
¼ cup water
60g butter
1½ cups (150g) stale wholemeal
   breadcrumbs

Combine yeast, honey and milk in medium bowl, mix well. Cover, stand in warm place for about 15 minutes, or until foamy. Sift flours into large bowl, stir in currants, make well in centre. Stir in combined egg, butter and yeast mixture, mix to a soft dough.

Turn dough onto lightly floured surface, knead until smooth. Place dough into lightly oiled bowl, cover, stand for about 40 minutes or until dough has doubled in size. Turn dough onto lightly floured surface, knead for 5 minutes or until smooth and elastic.

Divide dough in half, roll out each half into rectangle measuring 20cm x 25cm. Spread each rectangle evenly with half the caramel filling. Roll up dough from long sides like Swiss rolls, moisten ends of dough with water, pinch ends together. Place on lightly greased oven trays, allow room for spreading. Cover, stand in warm place for about 20 minutes or until increased in size by half. Slash tops of rolls in several places, bake in hot oven for 10 minutes, reduce heat to moderately hot, bake further 15 minutes or until golden brown. Stand on trays for 5 minutes before placing onto wire racks to cool. When cold, dust with sifted icing sugar.

Caramel Filling: Combine sugar and water in small saucepan, stir over high heat without boiling until sugar is dissolved. Bring to boil, boil rapidly, without stirring, for about 3 minutes or until mixture is slightly thickened. Remove from heat and stir in butter and breadcrumbs.

Makes 2.

From top: Apricot Spiral Teacake; Caramel Teacake Roll.

Cake stand: Studio-Haus; table and bowl: The Country Trader

ORANGE PARSNIP CAKE

You will need about 2 medium parsnips for this recipe. Cake can be made a day ahead; keep in airtight container. Cake can be frozen for 2 months. Recipe unsuitable to microwave.

125g butter
2 teaspoons grated orange rind
⅓ cup brown sugar
2 tablespoons orange juice
3 eggs
½ cup white self-raising flour
½ cup wholemeal self-raising flour
2 cups finely grated parsnip

Grease deep 20cm round cake pan, cover base with paper, grease paper. Cream butter, rind and sugar in small bowl with electric mixer until light and fluffy; add juice, beat until combined. Beat in eggs 1 at a time, beat until combined. Transfer mixture to large bowl, stir in sifted flours and parsnip in 2 batches. Spread mixture into prepared pan. Bake in moderate oven for about 1¼ hours or until firm. Stand 10 minutes before turning onto wire rack to cool.

PEAR AND GINGER LOAF

Loaf will keep for 3 days in airtight container, or loaf can be frozen for 2 months. This recipe is not suitable to microwave.

1¼ cups (200g) chopped dried pears
¼ cup chopped glacé ginger
½ cup water
½ cup brown sugar
15g butter
1¼ cups wholemeal self-raising flour
1 teaspoon ground ginger
½ teaspoon mixed spice
¾ cup slivered almonds

Grease 8cm x 26cm bar pan, line base with paper, grease paper. Combine pears, ginger, water, sugar and butter in medium saucepan, stir over low heat until butter is melted. Bring to boil, reduce heat; simmer, uncovered, for 2 minutes. Remove mixture from heat, cool to room temperature.

Sift flour and spices into large bowl, stir in pear mixture and ½ cup of the almonds. Spread mixture into prepared pan, sprinkle with remaining almonds. Bake in moderate oven for about 40 minutes or until golden brown. Turn loaf onto wire rack to cool.

From left: Orange Parsnip Cake; Pear and Ginger Loaf; Fig Bars.

Plates: The Antique General Store

FIG BARS

Bars can be made 3 days ahead; keep, covered, in refrigerator. They can be frozen for up to 2 months. Recipe unsuitable to microwave.

2 cups (350g) chopped dried figs
¾ cup apple juice
155g butter
¼ cup brown sugar
1 cup wholemeal plain flour
1 cup rolled oats
¼ cup chopped pecan nuts

Grease 19cm x 29cm lamington pan, line with paper, grease paper. Combine figs and juice in medium saucepan, bring to boil, reduce heat, cover, simmer for about 5 minutes or until figs are tender; cool.

Beat butter and sugar in small bowl with electric mixer until light and fluffy, stir in fig mixture. Add sifted flour, oats and nuts; mix well. Spread mixture into prepared pan. Bake in moderate oven for about 40 minutes or until golden brown, cool in pan.

HONEYED PINEAPPLE FRUIT CAKE

Cake can be made 1 month ahead; keep in airtight container or cake can be frozen for 2 months. Recipe unsuitable to microwave.

2 cups (320g) sultanas
2 cups (280g) currants
2 cups (440g) glacé cherries, halved
1 cup chopped raisins
¼ cup chopped glacé ginger
¼ cup honey
90g butter
2 cups unsweetened pineapple juice
1 cup soy milk
2 cups wholemeal plain flour
2 cups wholemeal self-raising flour
2 teaspoons mixed spice

Line deep 23cm square cake pan with 3 layers of greaseproof paper. Combine fruit, ginger, honey, butter and juice in large saucepan, stir over heat until butter is melted. Bring to boil, reduce heat, cover, simmer for 5 minutes. Transfer mixture to large bowl, cool to room temperature. Stir in milk, sifted flours and spice in 2 batches. Spread mixture evenly into prepared pan, bake in slow oven for about 3 hours; cover, cool in pan.

OREGANO CHEESE DAMPER

Damper is best made on day of serving, or damper can be frozen for 2 months. This recipe is not suitable to microwave.

1 cup wholemeal self-raising flour
1 cup white self-raising flour
60g butter
¼ cup chopped fresh oregano
½ cup grated tasty cheese
¾ cup milk
¼ cup water, approximately
1 tablespoon milk, extra
1 tablespoon grated parmesan cheese

Sift flours into large bowl, rub in butter, stir in oregano and tasty cheese. Make well in centre, add milk and enough water to mix to a sticky dough. Turn dough onto lightly floured surface, knead lightly until smooth. Shape into a round, place onto greased oven tray. Pat dough out to approximately 2cm thick and 20cm diameter. Using a sharp knife, mark into wedges about 1cm deep. Brush top with extra milk, sprinkle with parmesan cheese. Bake in moderately hot oven for about 25 minutes or until lightly browned.

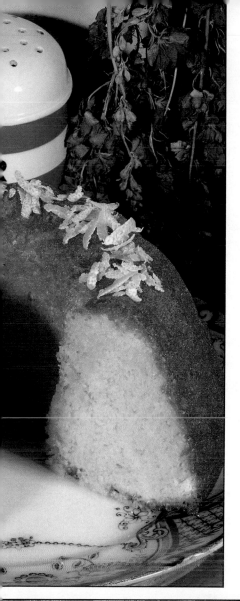

YOGHURT AND LEMON CAKE

Cake can be made 4 days ahead; keep in airtight container in refrigerator. This recipe is not suitable to freeze or microwave.

250g butter
2 teaspoons grated lemon rind
1 cup castor sugar
3 eggs, separated
½ cup coconut
¼ cup packaged ground almonds
2 tablespoons lemon juice
2½ cups white self-raising flour
200g carton plain yoghurt
HONEY SYRUP
1 medium lemon
1 cup honey

Grease 20cm baba pan. Cream butter, rind and sugar in small bowl with electric mixer until light and fluffy; beat in egg yolks one at a time. Transfer mixture to large bowl, stir in coconut, almonds and juice, then sifted flour and yoghurt in 2 batches.

Beat egg whites in small bowl until soft peaks form, fold into cake mixture. Pour into prepared pan, bake in moderate oven for about 1 hour or until firm. Spoon hot syrup mixture over hot cake; cool in pan.

Honey Syrup: Remove rind from lemon, cut rind into small pieces. Squeeze juice from lemon; you will need ¼ cup juice. Combine rind with juice and honey in small saucepan, stir over low heat until honey is melted; do not boil.

Accessories: Flossoms; table: Country Form (left)

SPICY BUTTERMILK CAKE

Cake can be made up to 3 days ahead; keep in airtight container, or freeze for 2 months. This recipe is not suitable to microwave.

125g butter
¾ cup brown sugar
3 eggs
1 cup white self-raising flour
1 cup wholemeal self-raising flour
1 teaspoon ground cinnamon
½ teaspoon ground cloves
½ teaspoon ground nutmeg
1 cup buttermilk
200g milk carob, melted
1 cup pecan nuts, chopped

Grease 23cm square slab pan, line with greaseproof paper, grease paper. Cream butter and sugar in small bowl with electric mixer until light and fluffy, beat in eggs 1 at a time, beat until combined. Stir in sifted dry ingredients and buttermilk in 2 batches.

Pour mixture into prepared pan, bake in moderate oven for about 35 minutes or until lightly browned. Stand 5 minutes before turning onto wire rack to cool. Spread cold cake with carob, sprinkle evenly with nuts.

BELOW: Honeyed Pineapple Fruit Cake.
LEFT: From left: Oregano Cheese Damper; Yoghurt and Lemon Cake.

WHOLEMEAL RAISIN PIKELETS

Batter can be prepared 2 hours ahead; cook pikelets just before serving. Pikelets can be frozen for 2 months. Recipe unsuitable to microwave.

½ cup wholemeal self-raising flour
½ cup white self-raising flour
¼ cup castor sugar
½ teaspoon ground cinnamon
1 egg
1 cup milk
1 teaspoon cider vinegar
15g butter, melted
½ cup chopped raisins

Sift flours, sugar and cinnamon into medium bowl, make well in centre. Gradually stir in combined egg, milk and vinegar, stir until smooth. Stir in butter and raisins.

Heat large heavy-based frying pan, lightly grease with butter. Drop dessertspoons of batter into pan from tip of spoon. When bubbles start to appear, turn pikelets and brown on other side.

Makes about 15.

ABOVE: From left: Tropical Fruit Teacake; Fruity Wholemeal Rock Cakes.
LEFT: Clockwise from left: Wholemeal Raisin Pikelets; Pumpkin Prune Scones; Spicy Buttermilk Cake.

PUMPKIN PRUNE SCONES

You will need to cook about 350g pumpkin for this recipe. Scones are best made on day of serving. Scones can be frozen for 2 months. Recipe unsuitable to microwave.

60g butter
¼ cup raw sugar
1 egg
1 cup cold mashed pumpkin
½ cup chopped pitted prunes
1½ cups white self-raising flour
1 cup wholemeal self-raising flour
½ teaspoon ground cinnamon

Grease 20cm sandwich pan. Beat butter and sugar in small bowl with electric mixer until light and fluffy, add egg, beat until combined. Stir in pumpkin, prunes and sifted flours and cinnamon, mix to a soft dough. Knead gently on floured surface until smooth.

Press dough out evenly until about 2cm thick, cut into rounds with 5cm cutter. Place rounds into prepared pan, brush tops lightly with a little milk. Bake in moderately hot oven for 25 minutes or until scones are lightly browned and sound hollow when tapped.

Makes about 10.

FRUITY WHOLEMEAL ROCK CAKES

Rock cakes are best made on day of serving, or can be frozen for 2 months. Cow's milk can be substituted for soy milk, if desired. Recipe unsuitable to microwave.

2 cups wholemeal self-raising flour
1 teaspoon mixed spice
125g butter
½ cup raw sugar
½ cup sultanas
½ cup chopped dates
2 tablespoons mixed peel
½ cup soy milk
1 egg, lightly beaten
2 tablespoons raw sugar, extra

Combine sifted flour and spice in large bowl, rub in butter, stir in sugar and fruit. Make well in centre, stir in combined milk and egg, mix until ingredients are just combined. Drop heaped tablespoons of mixture onto lightly greased oven trays, sprinkle with extra sugar, bake in moderately hot oven for about 15 minutes or until browned. Loosen rock cakes and cool on tray.

Makes about 15.

TROPICAL FRUIT TEACAKE

Cake can be made 2 days ahead. This recipe is not suitable to freeze or microwave.

60g butter
½ cup castor sugar
1 egg
½ cup white self-raising flour
½ cup wholemeal self-raising flour
⅓ cup milk
¾ cup Hawaiian mix
15g butter, melted, extra
2 teaspoons castor sugar, extra
½ teaspoon ground cinnamon

Grease 20cm sandwich pan, line base with paper, grease paper. Cream butter and sugar in small bowl with electric mixer until light and fluffy, beat in egg, beat until combined. Stir in sifted flours and milk in 2 batches. Stir in Hawaiian mix. Spread mixture into prepared pan, bake in moderate oven for about 30 minutes or until browned. Stand for 5 minutes before turning onto wire rack. Brush top with extra butter, sprinkle with combined extra sugar and cinnamon.

PUMPKIN AND HONEY LOAF

You will need to cook 200g pumpkin for this recipe. Loaf is best made on same day as serving. It can be frozen for 2 months. This recipe is not suitable to microwave.

1 cup white self-raising flour
1 cup wholemeal self-raising flour
½ teaspoon mixed spice
¼ teaspoon ground nutmeg
¼ teaspoon ground cloves
¼ teaspoon ground ginger
60g butter
½ cup cold mashed pumpkin
½ cup chopped dates
⅓ cup honey
¼ cup milk
1 egg, lightly beaten
2 tablespoons oil

Grease 14cm x 21cm loaf pan, line with greaseproof paper, grease paper. Sift flours and spices into large bowl, rub in butter. Stir in pumpkin, dates, honey, milk, egg and oil. Spread mixture into prepared pan. Bake in moderately slow oven for about 45 minutes or until firm. Stand for 5 minutes before turning onto wire rack to cool.

LEFT: From top: Apple Muffins; Pumpkin and Honey Loaf. RIGHT: From left: Corn and Peanut Butter Muffins; Carrot and Walnut Cake.

Basket, board and knife: The Country Trader (left); accessories: The Country Trader (right)

APPLE MUFFINS

Muffins are best made on day of serving. They can be frozen for 2 months. This recipe is not suitable to microwave.

½ cup wholemeal self-raising flour
½ cup white self-raising flour
¼ teaspoon ground cinnamon
¼ teaspoon ground nutmeg
60g butter
⅓ cup raw sugar
1 cup rolled oats
1 medium apple, grated
⅔ cup apple juice
2 eggs, lightly beaten

Grease 12 muffin pans. Sift flours and spices into a large bowl, rub in butter. Stir in sugar and oats. Make well in centre, stir in apple, juice and eggs with a fork, mix only until combined. Drop heaped tablespoons of mixture into prepared pans. Bake in moderately hot oven for about 20 minutes or until golden brown.

Makes 12.

CORN AND PEANUT BUTTER MUFFINS

Muffins are best cooked on day of serving. Muffins can be frozen for 2 months. This recipe is not suitable to microwave.

1½ cups wholemeal self-raising flour
1½ cups white self-raising flour
¼ cup castor sugar
60g butter
1 cup milk
300g can creamed corn
½ cup crunchy peanut butter
2 eggs, lightly beaten

Grease 12 deep muffin pans. Sift flours and sugar into large bowl, rub in butter; make well in centre. Combine remaining ingredients in medium bowl, add to flour mixture; mix with fork only until combined. Drop heaped tablespoons of mixture into prepared pans. Bake in moderately hot oven for about 20 minutes or until browned.

Makes 12.

CARROT AND WALNUT CAKE

You will need about 2 medium carrots for this recipe. Cake can be made up to 2 days ahead; keep in airtight container. Recipe unsuitable to freeze or microwave.

1½ cups white self-raising flour
1 teaspoon ground cinnamon
¾ cup raw sugar
2 cups grated carrot
½ cup sultanas
½ cup chopped walnuts
1 cup oil
4 eggs, lightly beaten

Grease 14cm x 21cm loaf pan, line base with paper, grease paper. Sift flour and cinnamon into large bowl, stir in sugar, carrot, sultanas and walnuts. Combine oil and eggs, stir into flour mixture. Pour mixture into prepared pan, bake in moderate oven for about 1 hour or until firm. Stand for 5 minutes before turning onto wire rack to cool.

PINEAPPLE DATE BARS

Bars can be made 2 days ahead; keep in airtight container. Bars can be frozen for a month. Recipe unsuitable to microwave.

¾ cup chopped dates
440g can unsweetened pineapple
**   pieces**
1 cup white self-raising flour
½ cup wholemeal plain flour
1 cup rolled oats
¼ cup brown sugar
½ cup shredded coconut
60g butter, melted
2 eggs, lightly beaten

Lightly grease 25cm x 30cm Swiss roll pan, place strip of greaseproof paper to cover base and extend over 2 opposite ends, grease paper. Combine dates and undrained pineapple pieces in small saucepan, bring to boil; reduce heat, simmer, uncovered, for 5 minutes. Remove from heat, drain, reserving ½ cup juice.

Combine pineapple mixture, sifted flours, oats, sugar and coconut in large bowl. Stir in combined butter, eggs and reserved juice. Spread mixture into prepared pan, bake in moderate oven for about 20 minutes or until golden brown, cool in pan.

BANANA MUESLI MUFFINS

Use microwave-proof muffin pan for microwave oven. Muffins can be frozen for 2 months. Cow's milk can be substituted for soy milk, if desired. You will need about 2 large bananas for these muffins.

1½ cups wholemeal self-raising flour
½ teaspoon ground nutmeg
½ cup untoasted muesli
⅓ cup wheatgerm
½ cup raw sugar
¾ cup mashed banana
90g butter, melted
2 eggs, lightly beaten
⅔ cup soy milk
2 tablespoons wheatgerm, extra

Grease 12 muffin pans. Combine sifted flour and nutmeg, muesli, wheatgerm and sugar in a large bowl. Stir in combined banana, butter, eggs and milk, mix with fork only until ingredients are just combined. Drop rounded tablespoons of mixture into prepared pans, sprinkle with extra wheatgerm, bake in moderately hot oven for about 20 minutes or until lightly browned (or microwave 6 muffins at a time on HIGH for about 3 minutes).

Makes 12.

Clockwise from top right: Peanut Butter Loaf; Pineapple Date Bars; Date and Citrus Bars; Banana Muesli Muffins.

DATE AND CITRUS BARS

Bars can be made 2 days ahead; keep in airtight container or freeze for 2 months. This recipe is unsuitable to microwave.

125g butter
½ cup brown sugar
¾ cup water
1 cup chopped dates
½ cup mixed peel
¾ cup wholemeal plain flour
¾ cup wholemeal self-raising flour
½ cup unprocessed bran
½ cup unsalted roasted peanuts
2 eggs, lightly beaten
1 teaspoon vanilla essence

Grease 25cm x 30cm Swiss roll pan, line base with paper, grease paper. Combine butter, sugar, water, dates and peel in medium saucepan, stir over heat, without boiling, until sugar is dissolved. Bring to boil, remove from heat; cool.

Sift flours into large bowl, add bran and peanuts; mix well. Stir in combined eggs, essence and date mixture. Spread mixture into prepared pan, bake in moderate oven for about 30 minutes or until golden brown.

PEANUT BUTTER LOAF

Loaf can be made 3 days ahead; keep in airtight container. Recipe unsuitable to freeze or microwave.

125g butter
½ cup honey
3 eggs
⅓ cup smooth peanut butter
1 cup white self-raising flour
¾ cup wholemeal plain flour
½ cup buttermilk

Grease deep 14cm x 21cm loaf pan, line base with paper, grease paper. Cream butter in small bowl with electric mixer until light and fluffy, add honey, beat well. Beat in eggs, 1 at a time, then beat in peanut butter. Transfer mixture to large bowl.

Stir in sifted flours and milk in 2 batches. Pour mixture into prepared pan, bake in moderate oven for about 30 minutes or until firm. Stand for 5 minutes before turning onto wire rack to cool.

RIGHT: From left: Caraway Biscuits; Apple Apricot Bars; Peanut Coconut Cookies. BELOW: From top: Apricot Muesli Biscuits; Oatmeal Apple Pikelets.

OATMEAL APPLE PIKELETS

Pikelets are best made on day of serving or can be frozen for 2 months. Recipe unsuitable to microwave.

1 cup white self-raising flour
1 teaspoon ground cinnamon
2 tablespoons brown sugar
⅔ cup rolled oats
1 egg, lightly beaten
1¼ cups soy milk
1 medium apple, grated
½ cup chopped walnuts

Sift flour and cinnamon into medium bowl, stir in sugar and oats. Make well in centre, gradually stir in combined egg and milk. Stir in apple and nuts. Cover, stand for 10 minutes.

Heat large heavy-based frying pan, lightly grease with butter. Drop tablespoons of mixture into pan from tip of spoon. When bubbles appear, turn pikelets over, cook until lightly browned underneath.

Makes about 20.

Serving ware: Flossoms; chest: Country Form (right); tin and can: Flossoms (below)

APRICOT MUESLI BISCUITS

Biscuits can be made 3 days ahead; keep in airtight container. They can be frozen for 2 months. Recipe unsuitable to microwave.

1 cup toasted apricot muesli
1 cup rolled oats
1 cup coconut
½ cup wholemeal self-raising flour
½ cup raw sugar
¼ cup sesame seeds
1 tablespoon golden syrup
1 egg, lightly beaten
185g butter, melted

Combine muesli, oats, coconut, flour, sugar and seeds in large bowl, make well in centre. Stir in combined golden syrup, egg and butter. Drop heaped teaspoons of mixture about 3cm apart onto lightly greased oven trays, press with fork. Bake in moderate oven for about 10 minutes or until golden brown. Cool on trays.

Makes about 45.

APRICOT APPLE BARS

Recipe can be made 2 days ahead; keep, covered, in refrigerator. Bars can be frozen for 2 months. Recipe unsuitable to microwave.

1 medium apple, grated
1½ cups wholemeal plain flour
1¼ cups (100g) rolled oats
¾ cup chopped dried apricots
½ cup slivered almonds
¼ cup sesame seeds
¼ cup honey
125g butter
1 teaspoon grated lemon rind
1 tablespoon lemon juice
1 tablespoon brown sugar

Grease 25cm x 30cm Swiss roll pan, line base with paper, grease paper. Squeeze excess moisture from apple. Sift flour into large bowl, stir in apple, oats, apricots, almonds and seeds; make well in centre. Combine honey, butter, rind, juice and sugar in small saucepan, stir over heat, without boiling, until sugar is dissolved, stir into flour mixture. Press mixture evenly into prepared pan. Bake in moderate oven for about 35 minutes or until golden brown. Cool in pan before cutting into bars.

CARAWAY BISCUITS

Biscuits can be kept for 2 weeks in airtight container. Recipe unsuitable to freeze or microwave.

125g butter
¼ cup brown sugar
2 tablespoons honey
1 egg, lightly beaten
1 tablespoon caraway seeds
1 cup wholemeal self-raising flour
1 cup white plain flour

Cream butter, sugar and honey in small bowl with electric mixer until light and fluffy. Add egg, beat until combined. Add seeds and sifted flours in 2 batches; mix to a firm dough. Turn dough onto lightly floured surface, knead lightly until smooth. Roll out to 3mm thickness, cut into 6cm rounds using a fluted cutter, place onto greased oven trays; prick each round with a fork. Bake in moderate oven for about 12 minutes or until lightly browned. Stand for 5 minutes before placing on wire racks to cool.

Makes about 24.

PEANUT COCONUT COOKIES

Cookies will keep for a week in airtight container. Cookies can also be frozen for up to 2 months. Recipe unsuitable to microwave.

90g butter
¼ cup smooth peanut butter
½ cup raw sugar
1 egg
1 cup wholemeal self-raising flour
1 cup coconut
½ cup unsalted roasted peanuts

Cream butter, peanut butter and sugar in small bowl with electric mixer until light and fluffy. Add egg, beat until just combined. Stir in flour, coconut and peanuts. Roll heaped teaspoons of mixture into balls, place about 2cm apart onto lightly greased oven trays, flatten slightly with fork. Bake in moderately hot oven for about 12 minutes or until lightly browned; cool on trays.

Makes about 30.

WHOLEGRAIN BREAD ROLLS

Rolls are best made on day of serving, or can be frozen for up to 2 months. Recipe unsuitable to microwave.

30g compressed yeast
1 tablespoon sugar
½ cup warm water
3 cups wholemeal plain flour
1 cup rye flour
¾ cup unprocessed bran
2 tablespoons wheatgerm
2 tablespoons sunflower seed kernels
2 tablespoons millet seeds
1¼ cups warm milk
1 tablespoon oil
1 tablespoon milk, extra

Lightly grease 2 x 15cm x 25cm loaf pans. Combine yeast, sugar and water in small bowl, cover, stand in warm place until foamy. Sift flours into large bowl, add bran, wheatgerm, kernels and seeds, mix well. Stir in yeast mixture and combined milk and oil, mix to a firm dough.

Turn dough onto floured surface, knead well for about 5 minutes or until smooth and elastic. Place dough into lightly oiled bowl, cover, stand in warm place for about 40 minutes or until dough is doubled in size.

Turn dough onto lightly floured surface, knead until smooth. Divide dough into 8 portions, shape into long rolls. Place 4 rolls crossways in each pan. Cover, stand in warm place for about 40 minutes or until doubled in size. Brush rolls lightly with extra milk, bake in moderately hot oven for about 30 minutes or until rolls are browned and sound hollow when tapped.

Makes 8.

FRUITY BRAN LOAF

Loaf can be made a day ahead; keep, covered, in airtight container. Loaf can be frozen for 2 months; slice bread before freezing and take out slices as required. This recipe is not suitable to microwave.

2½ cups wholemeal self-raising flour
2½ cups white self-raising flour
1 teaspoon mixed spice
2 teaspoons ground cinnamon
2 cups (320g) oat bran
15g butter
2 tablespoons golden syrup
¾ cup water
½ cup sultanas
½ cup chopped raisins
½ cup chopped dried apricots
1½ cups soy milk

Grease 2 x 14cm x 21cm loaf pans. Sift flours and spices into large bowl, stir in bran; make well in centre. Combine butter, golden syrup, water and fruit in medium saucepan, stir over heat until butter is melted. Remove from heat, stir in soy milk. Stir liquid into dry ingredients, mix to a firm dough (you may need a little extra soy milk).

Turn dough onto lightly floured surface, divide in half. Knead each half until smooth, place both halves into 1 of the prepared pans. Place remaining pan over dough so it is enclosed. Use 2 large "bulldog" clips to hold the loaf pans together, or, after placing pans into the oven, weight the top pan with a brick.

Bake in moderate oven for 1¼ hours, remove top pan, return bread to oven for about 20 minutes or until it sounds hollow when tapped and is well browned. Turn onto wire rack to cool.

CHIVE AND CORN BREAD

Bread is best when freshly cooked. This recipe is not suitable to freeze or microwave.

½ cup white self-raising flour
½ cup wholemeal self-raising flour
¾ cup polenta
1 tablespoon sugar
½ cup chopped fresh chives
½ cup sour cream
½ cup plain yoghurt
60g butter, melted
2 tablespoons milk
1 egg, lightly beaten

Lightly grease 8cm x 26cm bar pan, line with paper, grease paper. Sift flours into large bowl, add polenta, sugar and chives, mix well. Make well in centre, stir in combined remaining ingredients. Spread mixture evenly into prepared pan. Bake in moderately hot oven for about 25 minutes or until lightly browned. Turn onto wire rack to cool slightly before serving.

RYE AND WALNUT ROLLS

Rolls can be made 2 days ahead; keep in airtight container, or freeze for up to 2 months. This recipe is not suitable to microwave.

7g sachet dry yeast
½ cup warm soy milk
2 teaspoons treacle
1 cup rye flour
1½ cups white plain flour
¾ cup wholemeal plain flour
½ cup chopped walnuts
1 cup apple juice
1 egg, lightly beaten
1 tablespoon chopped walnuts, extra

Combine yeast, milk and treacle in small bowl, cover; stand in warm place until foamy. Sift flours into large bowl, add walnuts; make well in centre. Stir in yeast mixture and apple juice, mix to a soft dough. Turn dough onto lightly floured surface, knead well for about 5 minutes. Place dough in lightly oiled bowl, stand, covered, in warm place for about 40 minutes, or until dough has doubled in size.

Turn dough onto lightly floured surface, knead well.

Divide dough into 12 portions, roll each portion into a ball, place close together on lightly greased oven tray.

Cover, stand in warm place for about 30 minutes or until doubled in size. Brush lightly with egg, sprinkle with extra walnuts. Bake in moderately hot oven for about 20 minutes or until lightly browned.

Makes 12.

ABOVE: Clockwise from left: Wholegrain Bread Rolls; Fruity Bran Loaf; Chive and Corn Bread; Rye and Walnut Rolls.

Accessories: The Country Trader

101

Everyone will enjoy these easy-to-eat morsels, whether you serve them after dinner, between times or in school lunches

APRICOT AND RICOTTA DATES

Recipe can be made a day ahead; keep, covered, in refrigerator. Recipe unsuitable to freeze.

12 fresh dates, pitted
FILLING
125g ricotta cheese
2 tablespoons chopped dried apricots
2 tablespoons packaged ground almonds
1 tablespoon castor sugar
½ teaspoon vanilla essence
½ teaspoon grated orange rind
Fill dates with ricotta cheese mixture, refrigerate. Slice dates before serving.
Filling: Combine all ingredients in a medium bowl; mix well.
Makes 36.

FRUIT AND NUT CAROB CLUSTERS

Clusters can be made 2 days ahead; keep, covered, in refrigerator. Recipe unsuitable to freeze.

150g milk carob, melted
1 cup chopped dates
½ cup chopped glacé apricots
½ cup roasted hazelnuts
2 tablespoons coconut
Combine carob, dates, apricots and hazelnuts in medium bowl; mix well. Drop heaped teaspoons of mixture onto foil-covered tray, sprinkle with coconut; refrigerate until set.
Makes about 24.

CAROB SESAME ROUNDS

Sweets can be made 2 days ahead; keep, covered, in refrigerator. Recipe unsuitable to freeze.

2 tablespoons sesame seeds
1¼ cups (115g) coconut
2 tablespoons carob powder
2 tablespoons honey
⅓ cup orange juice
extra coconut
Stir seeds over medium heat in heavy-based pan until lightly browned. Remove from pan to cool.
Process seeds, coconut, carob, honey and juice until well combined. Roll mixture into small balls, toss in extra coconut, refrigerate until firm.
Makes about 35.

From left: Apricot and Ricotta Dates; Fruit and Nut Carob Clusters; Carob Sesame Rounds.

Tin, plate and rack: Flossoms; chest: Country Form

Dinner Party for 2

Colourful and tasty vegetarian dishes fit perfectly into a smart dinner party, and are simple to prepare. These servings are generous for 2 people, and we give you do-ahead tips to make preparation easy.

MENU

Soup
Pumpkin Walnut Soup

Entrée
Nutty Lentil Pastries

Main Course
Baked Eggplant with Cheesy Peppers
Snow Pea Salad with Chilli Dressing

Dessert
Rhubarb Soufflés with Citrus Strawberries

PUMPKIN WALNUT SOUP

Soup can be made a day ahead; keep, covered, in refrigerator. Soup can be frozen for 2 months.

15g butter
1 medium onion, chopped
1 clove garlic, crushed
300g pumpkin, chopped
1½ cups water
1 large vegetable stock cube, crumbled
2 teaspoons tomato paste
2 tablespoons chopped walnuts

Melt butter in medium saucepan, add onion and garlic, stir over medium heat for about 2 minutes (or microwave on HIGH for about 3 minutes) or until onion is soft. Add pumpkin, water, stock cube, paste and walnuts, bring to boil, reduce heat, cover, simmer for about 30 minutes (or microwave on HIGH for about 10 minutes) or until pumpkin is tender. Blend or process pumpkin mixture until smooth. Reheat before serving.

Clockwise from top: Rhubarb Soufflés with Citrus Strawberries; Snow Pea Salad with Chilli Dressing; Baked Eggplant with Cheesy Peppers; Nutty Lentil Pastries; Pumpkin Walnut Soup.

China and cutlery: Limoges; table and chair: Wentworth Antiques

NUTTY LENTIL PASTRIES

Pastries can be prepared a day ahead; keep, covered, in refrigerator. Recipe unsuitable to freeze or microwave.

3 sheets fillo pastry
45g butter, melted
2 teaspoons sesame seeds
NUTTY LENTIL FILLING
2 teaspoons butter
3 green shallots, chopped
1 clove garlic, crushed
1½ teaspoons chopped fresh basil
2 tablespoons red lentils
⅔ cup water
¼ cup brazil nuts, finely chopped
¼ cup lentil sprouts

Layer the pastry sheets together, brushing each with melted butter. Cut pastry crossways into 6 equal strips.

STEP 1
Divide filling into 6 portions, place 1 portion onto 1 end of each strip.

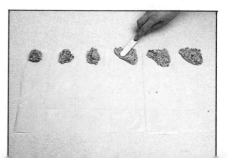

STEP 2

Fold corner of pastry over filling to form triangle. Lift first triangle up and over, keeping triangle shape.

Continue folding over to end of pastry strip, trim any excess pastry. Place triangles onto lightly greased oven tray. Brush lightly with butter, sprinkle with seeds. Bake in moderately hot oven for about 15 minutes or until lightly browned.

Nutty Lentil Filling: Melt butter in small saucepan, add shallots and garlic, stir over medium heat for about 1 minute (or microwave on HIGH for about 1 minute) or until shallots are soft. Stir in basil, lentils and water, bring to boil, reduce heat, partly cover, simmer for about 25 minutes (or microwave on HIGH for about 15 minutes) or until lentils are soft and mixture is thick. Remove from heat, stir in nuts, cool, stir in sprouts.

Makes 6.

BAKED EGGPLANT WITH CHEESY PEPPERS

Tomato sauce can be made a day ahead; keep, covered, in refrigerator. Eggplant is best baked just before serving. Recipe unsuitable to freeze.

1 medium eggplant
salt
2 tablespoons olive oil
1 medium red pepper, chopped
½ medium green pepper, chopped
1 clove garlic, crushed
1 sprig rosemary
1 tablespoon chopped fresh basil
2 teaspoons chopped fresh oregano
250g ricotta cheese
½ cup grated mozzarella cheese
2 tablespoons grated parmesan cheese
TOMATO SAUCE
15g butter
1 small onion, chopped
1 clove garlic, crushed
1 tablespoon white plain flour
1 cup tomato juice
1 teaspoon chopped fresh basil
½ teaspoon chopped fresh oregano
1 teaspoon brown sugar

Halve eggplant lengthways, remove flesh leaving 1cm shell; chop flesh. Place flesh into colander, sprinkle with salt; sprinkle inside of eggplant shells with salt, stand for 20 minutes. Rinse flesh and shells under cold water, drain; pat dry with absorbent paper.

Heat oil in large frying pan, add peppers, garlic and rosemary, stir over medium heat for about 5 minutes (or microwave on HIGH for about 5 minutes) or until peppers are soft. Stir in chopped eggplant, basil and oregano, stir over medium heat for about 5 minutes (or microwave on HIGH for about 3 minutes) or until eggplant is soft, remove from heat; remove rosemary. Stir in ricotta, half the mozzarella and half the parmesan.

Spoon mixture into eggplant shells, place shells on oven tray, sprinkle with remaining mozzarella and parmesan. Bake in moderate oven for about 25 minutes (or microwave on HIGH for about 5 minutes) or until shells are tender and filling is heated through. Serve with tomato sauce.

Tomato Sauce: Melt butter in medium saucepan, add onion and garlic, stir over medium heat for about 2 minutes (or microwave on HIGH for about 2 minutes) or until onion is soft. Stir in flour, stir over medium heat for 1 minute (or microwave on HIGH for 1 minute). Gradually stir in juice, basil, oregano and sugar, stir over heat (or microwave on HIGH for 3 minutes) until mixture boils and thickens.

ABOVE: Nutty Lentil Pastries. RIGHT: Rhubarb Soufflés with Citrus Strawberries.

SNOW PEA SALAD WITH CHILLI DRESSING

Prepare salad just before serving. Dressing can be made a day ahead; keep, covered, in refrigerator. Recipe unsuitable to freeze.

100g snow peas
½ butter lettuce
1 small long thin green cucumber, sliced
½ cup cherry tomatoes
1 small onion, sliced
CHILLI DRESSING
¼ cup olive oil
2 tablespoons cider vinegar
1 small fresh red chilli, finely chopped
1 tablespoon chopped fresh parsley
1 clove garlic, crushed
¼ teaspoon sugar

Steam or microwave snow peas until just tender, drain; rinse under cold water, drain. Combine lettuce, cucumber, tomatoes, onion and snow peas in a bowl, add dressing and toss gently.

Chilli Dressing: Combine all ingredients in jar, shake well.

RHUBARB SOUFFLES WITH CITRUS STRAWBERRIES

Strawberries can be prepared a day ahead; keep, covered, in refrigerator. Make soufflés just before serving. This recipe is unsuitable to freeze or microwave.

125g fresh or frozen rhubarb
¼ cup water
1 tablespoon cornflour
2 tablespoons castor sugar
1 egg, separated
2 egg whites
CITRUS STRAWBERRIES
2 tablespoons castor sugar
¼ cup water
½ teaspoon grated orange rind
¼ cup orange juice
½ x 250g punnet strawberries, halved

Combine rhubarb and water in medium saucepan, bring to boil, reduce heat, cover, simmer for about 10 minutes or until rhubarb is soft. Blend or process rhubarb mixture until smooth; push mixture through sieve then return to saucepan.

Combine cornflour, sugar and egg yolk in small bowl, stir until smooth. Stir cornflour mixture into rhubarb pureé, stir over high heat until mixture boils and thickens, remove from heat, cool 5 minutes. Add 1 egg white to mixture, whisk until combined; transfer mixture to large bowl.

Beat remaining egg whites in small bowl until firm peaks form, gently fold into rhubarb mixture in 2 batches. Pour mixture into 2 greased ovenproof dishes (½ cup capacity). Place dishes in small baking dish, pour in enough boiling water to come halfway up sides of dishes. Bake in moderate oven for 30 minutes. Serve soufflés immediately with strawberries.

Citrus Strawberries: Combine sugar and water in small saucepan, stir over high heat, without boiling, until sugar is dissolved, bring to boil, boil, uncovered, without stirring, for 4 minutes. Stir in rind and juice, cool mixture to room temperature. Add strawberries, cover and refrigerate until cool.

Here's a terrific variety of tastes and textures, followed by a refreshing bombe and rich truffles.

MENU
Entrée
Country Mushroom Pâté

Main Course
Herbed Nut Loaf with Pimiento Sauce
Sautéed Garlic Potatoes
Cauliflower Fritters with Tahini Sauce
Artichokes with Vegetables Julienne
Wholemeal Poppyseed Damper

Dessert
Grapefruit and Apricot Bombe
Peppermint Truffles

COUNTRY MUSHROOM PATE

Pâté can be made 2 days ahead; keep, covered in refrigerator. This recipe is unsuitable to freeze or microwave.

60g butter
1 medium onion, chopped
1 clove garlic, crushed
500g mushrooms, sliced
⅔ cup stale wholemeal breadcrumbs
125g cottage cheese
1 tablespoon lemon juice
1 tablespoon chopped fresh parsley

Melt butter in large frying pan, add onion and garlic, stir over medium heat for about 2 minutes or until onion is soft. Stir in mushrooms, reduce heat, cover, cook gently for about 10 minutes. Remove lid, bring to boil, boil until liquid has evaporated; cool.

Blend or process mushroom mixture with remaining ingredients until smooth. Transfer mixture to serving dish. Cover, refrigerate for several hours. Serve with wholemeal melba toast and crunchy fresh vegetables, if desired.

HERBED NUT LOAF WITH PIMIENTO SAUCE

Loaf can be prepared 3 hours before baking. Sauce can be made 2 days ahead; keep, covered, in refrigerator. This recipe is unsuitable to freeze or microwave.

30g butter
1 large onion, finely chopped
1½ tablespoons white plain flour
1 cup skim milk
2 egg whites
1½ cups (200g) unsalted cashew nuts, finely ground
¾ cup brazil nuts, finely ground
2 cups (200g) stale wholemeal breadcrumbs
¼ cup grated tasty cheese
1 tablespoon chopped fresh parsley
HERB SEASONING
2 cups (200g) stale wholemeal breadcrumbs
4 green shallots, chopped
1 teaspoon chopped fresh thyme
1 teaspoon chopped fresh rosemary
1 teaspoon chopped fresh sage
2 tablespoons chopped fresh parsley
2 tablespoons chopped fresh chives
¼ teaspoon ground nutmeg
2 egg yolks
90g butter, melted
PIMIENTO SAUCE
30g butter
1 small onion, chopped
1 clove garlic, crushed
400g can pimientos, drained, chopped
3 teaspoons sugar
¾ cup water
2 teaspoons lemon juice

Lightly grease 15cm x 25cm loaf pan, line base with paper, grease paper. Melt butter in medium saucepan, add onion, stir over medium heat for about 2 minutes (or microwave on HIGH for about 3 minutes) or until onion is soft. Stir in flour, stir over medium heat for 1 minute (or microwave on HIGH for 1 minute).

Remove from heat, gradually stir in milk, stir over high heat (or microwave on HIGH for about 2 minutes) until mixture boils and thickens; cool, stir in egg whites, nuts, breadcrumbs, cheese and parsley.

Spread half mixture into prepared pan. Top evenly with herb seasoning, then remaining nut mixture, press lightly to level surface. Bake in moderate oven for about 1 hour or until firm. Stand for 5 minutes before turning onto plate; sprinkle with extra grated cheese, if desired. Serve sliced with pimiento sauce.

Herb Seasoning: Combine all ingredients in medium bowl, mix well.
Pimiento Sauce: Melt butter in small saucepan, add onion and garlic, stir over medium heat for about 2 minutes (or microwave on HIGH for about 2 minutes) or until onion is soft. Add pimientos, sugar, water and juice, bring to boil, reduce heat, simmer, uncovered, for 1 minute. Blend or process mixture until smooth.

ABOVE: From left: Herbed Nut Loaf with Pimiento Sauce; Artichokes with Vegetables Julienne.

SAUTEED GARLIC POTATOES

Potatoes can be cooked several hours ahead; keep, covered, in refrigerator. This recipe is unsuitable to freeze or microwave.

1½kg baby new potatoes, halved
90g butter
1 tablespoon oil
2 cloves garlic, crushed
1 tablespoon grated lemon rind
2 tablespoons chopped fresh parsley

Boil, steam or microwave potatoes until just tender; drain well. Heat butter and oil in large frying pan, add garlic and potatoes, stir over medium heat for about 8 minutes or until potatoes are golden brown. Remove potatoes from pan, combine in large bowl with rind and parsley, toss gently.

CAULIFLOWER FRITTERS WITH TAHINI SAUCE

Fritters are best made just before serving. Sauce can be made a day ahead; keep, covered, in refrigerator. This recipe is unsuitable to freeze or microwave.

½ medium cauliflower, chopped
BATTER
1 cup white plain flour
2 tablespoons oil
½ teaspoon sesame oil
¾ cup water
1 egg white
oil for deep-frying
TAHINI SAUCE
3 tablespoons tahini
¼ cup lemon juice
1 tablespoon water
2 tablespoons oil
1 tablespoon chopped fresh parsley

Boil steam or microwave cauliflower until just tender; drain, cool.

Batter: Sift flour into medium bowl, make well in centre. Gradually stir in combined oils and water, mix to a smooth batter. Beat egg white in small bowl until firm peaks form, fold into batter. Dip cauliflower pieces into batter, deep-fry in hot oil until lightly browned; drain on absorbent paper. Serve with sauce.
Tahini Sauce: Combine all ingredients in a small bowl, mix well.

ARTICHOKES WITH VEGETABLE JULIENNE

Vegetable and dressing can be prepared a day ahead; keep, covered, in refrigerator. This recipe is unsuitable to freeze.

400g can artichoke bottoms, drained
1 medium carrot
1 medium red pepper
100g green beans
CHEESY DRESSING
2 egg yolks
2 tablespoons ricotta cheese
2 tablespoons grated tasty cheese
1 tablespoon orange juice
1 teaspoon seeded mustard
2 teaspoons chopped fresh thyme
½ cup olive oil

Cut artichokes, carrot and pepper into thin strips about 5cm long. Cut beans into 5cm pieces. Boil, steam or microwave beans and carrots until just tender; cool. Combine all vegetables in dish. Serve with dressing.
Cheesy Dressing: Blend or process egg yolks, cheeses, juice, mustard and thyme until smooth. Add oil gradually, while motor is operating, until mixture is thickened.

WHOLEMEAL POPPYSEED DAMPER

Make damper as close to serving time as possible. Damper can be frozen for 2 months. Recipe unsuitable to microwave.

3 cups wholemeal self-raising flour
1 tablespoon poppy seeds
2 tablespoons oil
1⅓ cups buttermilk, approximately

Sift flour into large bowl, add poppy seeds, mix well, make well in centre. Stir in oil and enough buttermilk to mix to a sticky dough. Turn dough onto lightly floured surface, knead until smooth and round.

Place dough onto lightly greased oven tray, pat firmly until about 4cm thick. Using a sharp knife, cut a cross in the top about 1cm deep. Brush top with a little milk, sprinkle with extra poppy seeds, if desired. Bake in moderately hot oven for about 40 minutes or until golden brown.

GRAPEFRUIT AND APRICOT BOMBE

Bombe is best made a day ahead; keep, covered, in freezer.

3 large grapefruit
1⅓ cups castor sugar
500g fresh apricots, chopped
2 cups milk

Peel and segment grapefruit, discard seeds. Combine grapefruit segments and 1 cup of the sugar in food processor, process until smooth. Pour mixture into lamington pan, cover with foil, freeze for about 2 hours or until mixture is firm.

Flake mixture with a fork, press evenly over base and side of well-chilled aluminium pudding steamer (6 cup capacity), cover, freeze until firm.

Process remaining sugar, apricots and milk until smooth. Pour into centre of steamer, cover, freeze until firm.

To serve, dip base of steamer into hot water, turn onto dish.

PEPPERMINT TRUFFLES

Truffles can be made 2 days ahead; keep, covered, in refrigerator. Recipe unsuitable to freeze.

200g milk carob, melted
¼ cup cream
⅓ cup sultanas
⅓ cup packaged ground hazelnuts
peppermint essence
¾ cup chopped roasted hazelnuts

Combine carob, cream, sultanas and ground hazelnuts in medium bowl, stir in essence to taste, cover, refrigerate for 30 minutes. Roll heaped teaspoons of mixture into balls, toss in chopped hazelnuts, cover, refrigerate until firm. Serve in foil cups, if desired.

Makes about 30.

ABOVE: From top: Peppermint Truffles; Grapefruit and Apricot Bombe.

China and table: The Country Trader; fabric: Boyac.

Buffet Dinner for 20

The food is fabulous in this lavish menu, with dishes reflecting the influence of Indian cuisine; they are all particularly easy for your guests to help themselves.

MENU

Entree
Spicy Split Pea Bundles

Main Course
Carrot Kofta with Lentil Sauce
Coconut Pilaf
Lentil Dhal
Chick Pea Salad with Chilli Lime Dressing
Broccoli and Potato in Spicy Coriander Sauce
Mushroom and Bean Salad

Accompaniments
Pineapple Sambal
Coconut and Chilli Sambal
Tomato Cucumber Relish
Chapatis
Pappadams

Dessert
Fresh Fruit with Ginger Yoghurt Sauce
Berry Coconut Trifle

SPICY SPLIT PEA BUNDLES

Bundles are best made close to serving time. Filling can be made a day ahead; keep, covered, in refrigerator. This recipe is unsuitable to freeze or microwave.

21 sheets fillo pastry
125g butter, melted
SPICY SPLIT PEA FILLING
2 cups (400g) yellow split peas
60g butter
1 large onion, chopped
2 cloves garlic, crushed
1 tablespoon grated fresh ginger
2 small fresh red chillies, chopped
2 medium tomatoes, peeled, chopped
2 tablespoons tomato paste
1 tablespoon lemon juice
2 tablespoons chopped fresh coriander

Place 1 sheet pastry on bench, cover remaining pastry with greaseproof paper, then a damp cloth to prevent drying. Brush pastry lightly with butter, top with another sheet of pastry, brush with butter, top with 1 more sheet of pastry. Cut pastry into 6 equal squares, place level tablespoon of filling into centre of each square. Pull up edges of pastry, enclosing filling, carefully twist top into a bundle. Repeat with remaining pastry, butter and filling.

Place bundles onto greased oven trays, brush lightly with butter; bake in moderate oven for about 10 minutes or until golden brown.

Spicy Split Pea Filling: Place peas in large bowl, cover well with cold water, soak overnight.

Next day, add split peas to large saucepan of boiling water, boil, uncovered, for about 20 minutes or until tender; drain. Melt butter in large saucepan, add onion, garlic and ginger, stir over medium heat for about 3 minutes or until onion is soft. Stir in chillies, tomatoes, paste, juice and split peas. Bring to boil, reduce heat, simmer, uncovered, for about 5 minutes, stirring occasionally, or until mixture is thick; cool. Stir in coriander.

Makes 42.

Spicy Split Pea Bundles.

Fabric: Gallery Nomad

Screen, brass tray, dessert table, artefacts: Indian Tourist Bureau; copper & brass serving ware: The Brass Man; table: The Country Trader; background fabric & ladle: Gallery Nomad

BACK RIGHT CORNER: *From top: Fresh Fruit with Ginger Yoghurt Sauce; Berry Coconut Trifle.* **BACK ROW:** *From left: Broccoli and*

Potato in Spicy Coriander Sauce; Coconut Pilaf; Lentil Dhal; Pineapple Sambal. **CENTRE ROW:** *From left: Mushroom and Bean*

Salad; Chick Pea Salad with Chilli Lime Dressing; Coconut and
Chilli Sambal; Tomato Cucumber Relish; Chapatis; Pappadams.

FRONT ROW: From left: Carrot Kofta with Lentil Sauce; Spicy
Split Pea Bundles.

CARROT KOFTA WITH LENTIL SAUCE

Recipe can be prepared several hours ahead; keep, covered, in refrigerator. Recipe unsuitable to freeze.

2kg carrots, finely grated
2 cups white plain flour
2 teaspoons ground coriander
½ teaspoon cayenne pepper
2 eggs, lightly beaten
LENTIL SAUCE
125g butter
2 medium onions, chopped
2 cloves garlic, crushed
⅓ cup chopped fresh coriander
1 tablespoon garam masala
2 teaspoons ground turmeric
½ teaspoon cayenne pepper
2 cups (400g) dried red lentils
2 x 415ml cans tomato purée
2½ litres (10 cups) water
1 large vegetable stock cube, crumbled

Combine carrots, flour, spices and eggs in large bowl; mix well. Divide mixture into about 40 equal portions, shape into balls. Place balls on tray, cover, refrigerate 30 minutes. Add 6 balls at a time to large saucepan of simmering water, simmer for about 10 minutes or until heated through. Remove with slotted spoon, drain on absorbent paper; keep warm. Repeat with remaining balls. Serve with sauce.
Lentil Sauce: Melt butter in large saucepan, add onions, garlic, coriander and spices, stir over medium heat for about 3 minutes (or microwave on HIGH for about 4 minutes) or until onions are soft. Stir in lentils, stir over medium heat for 2 minutes (or microwave on HIGH for 1 minute), stir in remaining ingredients. Bring to boil, reduce heat, simmer, uncovered, for about 30 minutes (or microwave on HIGH for about 20 minutes), or until lentils are soft.

COCONUT PILAF

Prepare pilaf close to serving time. This recipe is not suitable to freeze or microwave.

2 tablespoons flaked coconut
3¾ cups (750g) Basmati rice
2 x 340ml cans coconut milk
3½ cups water
pinch saffron powder
½ cup raisins
2 tablespoons oil
2 teaspoons cumin seeds
2 tablespoons sesame seeds
½ cup unroasted unsalted cashew nuts

Stir coconut over medium heat in heavy-based pan until lightly browned. Remove from pan to cool.

Wash rice in cold water several times until water is clear; drain. Combine rice, coconut milk, water and saffron in large saucepan, stir over high heat until mixture boils. Add raisins, reduce heat, partly cover, simmer for about 10 minutes or until most of the liquid is absorbed. Cover, cook over very low heat for further 10 minutes. Remove from heat, leave covered in saucepan.

Heat oil in large frying pan, add seeds and nuts, stir over medium heat until lightly browned. Stir into rice mixture. Spoon hot rice into dish, sprinkle with toasted coconut.

LENTIL DHAL

Dhal can be made a day ahead; keep, covered, in refrigerator. Recipe unsuitable to freeze or microwave.

2½ cups (500g) brown lentils
30g butter
2 medium onions, finely chopped
2 small fresh red chillies, finely chopped
1 teaspoon ground cumin
1 teaspoon ground coriander
½ teaspoon garam masala
½ teaspoon ground cardamom
1½ litres (6 cups) water
1 large vegetable stock cube, crumbled
1 teaspoon ground turmeric

Place lentils in large bowl, cover with water, stand overnight; drain. Melt butter in large saucepan, add onions, chillies, cumin, coriander, garam masala and cardamom, stir over medium heat for about 2 minutes or until onions are just soft. Stir in lentils and combined water, stock cube and turmeric, bring to boil, reduce heat, simmer, uncovered, for about 50 minutes or until mixture is thick.

CHICK PEA SALAD WITH CHILLI LIME DRESSING

Salad can be prepared several hours ahead; keep, covered, in refrigerator. This recipe is not suitable to freeze or microwave.

1½ cups (315g) dried chick peas
1 lettuce
2 medium green peppers, chopped
2 medium red peppers, chopped
2 medium cucumbers, chopped
5 medium tomatoes, chopped
10 small radishes, chopped
1 medium onion, sliced
CHILLI LIME DRESSING
⅔ cup lime juice
1 tablespoon sugar
⅓ cup chopped fresh coriander
1 small fresh red chilli, chopped

Place chick peas in large bowl, cover with water; stand overnight.

Next day, drain chick peas. Add chick peas to large saucepan of boiling water, cover, simmer for about 1 hour or until tender, drain; cool.

Combine chick peas in large bowl with remaining ingredients. Line large serving bowl with lettuce leaves, top with chick pea mixture. Pour dressing over salad just before serving.
Chilli Lime Dressing: Combine all ingredients in a jar; shake well.

BROCCOLI AND POTATO IN SPICY CORIANDER SAUCE

Recipe can be made several hours ahead; keep, covered, in refrigerator. This recipe is not suitable to freeze or microwave.

2 tablespoons oil
3 teaspoons cumin seeds
3 teaspoons ground coriander
½ teaspoon paprika
1kg broccoli, chopped
4 medium potatoes, chopped
4 medium tomatoes, peeled, chopped
¼ cup tomato paste
2 tablespoons chopped fresh coriander

Heat oil in large saucepan, add seeds, ground coriander and paprika, stir over medium heat for 1 minute. Add broccoli and potatoes, stir over medium heat for 1 minute. Blend or process tomatoes and paste until smooth, add to broccoli mixture. Bring to boil, reduce heat, simmer gently, uncovered, for about 20 minutes or until potatoes are tender, stirring occasionally. Stir in fresh coriander just before serving.

MUSHROOM AND BEAN SALAD

Salad can be made several hours ahead; keep, covered, in refrigerator. Recipe unsuitable to freeze.

1 cup sultanas
750g baby mushrooms, sliced
500g green beans, sliced
1 medium red pepper, sliced
½ cup chopped fresh parsley
¾ cup shredded coconut
½ cup oil
2 tablespoons yellow mustard seeds
¼ cup sesame seeds
⅓ cup lemon juice

Place sultanas in a small bowl, cover with boiling water.

Combine mushrooms, beans, pepper, parsley and coconut in large bowl. Heat oil in a small saucepan, add mustard seeds and stir over medium heat until seeds begin to pop. Stir in sesame seeds, stir over medium heat until lightly browned. Add to mushroom mixture with juice and drained sultanas, toss gently.

PINEAPPLE SAMBAL

Sambal can be prepared several hours ahead; keep, covered, in refrigerator. Recipe unsuitable to freeze.

1 medium pineapple, chopped
½ cup chopped fresh mint
2 teaspoons grated fresh ginger
Combine all ingredients in medium bowl. Refrigerate before serving.

COCONUT AND CHILLI SAMBAL

Sambal can be prepared a day ahead; keep, covered, in refrigerator. Recipe unsuitable to freeze.

2 cups (180g) coconut
2 tablespoons lime juice
6 dried red chillies, chopped
4 cloves garlic, crushed
1 cup plain yoghurt
Blend or process all ingredients until combined. Serve at room temperature.

TOMATO CUCUMBER RELISH

Relish can be made a day ahead; keep, covered, in refrigerator. This recipe is unsuitable to freeze.

1 medium onion, chopped
1 small green cucumber, chopped
2 medium tomatoes, chopped
2 tablespoons chopped fresh coriander
4 small fresh green chillies, chopped
1 tablespoon lime juice
¼ teaspoon ground cumin
¼ teaspoon ground coriander
Combine all ingredients in medium bowl; mix well. Refrigerate for 2 hours before serving.

CHAPATIS

Prepare chapatis close to serving time. This recipe is not suitable to freeze or microwave.

3 cups white plain flour
1 cup wholemeal plain flour
2 teaspoons caraway seeds
125g butter
1⅓ cups hot water
ghee

Sift flours into large bowl, stir in seeds, rub in butter; make well in centre. Gradually add water, mix to a soft dough. Turn dough onto unfloured surface, knead until dough is smooth and elastic. Cut dough in half, cut each half into 10 even portions. Knead each portion well. Roll each piece of dough into a long thin sausage, roll up into a coil, flatten with hand. Roll coil out to a 15cm round.

Heat heavy-based frying pan over medium heat, lightly grease with ghee. Cook chapatis 1 at a time. Press edge of chapati lightly with a clean cloth during cooking to encourage it to rise. When golden brown patches appear on bottom, turn and cook other side until golden brown, pressing edge with cloth. Repeat with remaining chapatis.

Makes 20.

PAPPADAMS

Pappadams can be cooked several hours ahead; keep in airtight container. Recipe unsuitable to freeze.

oil for shallow-frying
20 large pappadams
Heat 2cm oil in heavy-based frying pan. Add pappadams 1 at a time. Hold under oil with tongs for about 3 seconds, turn, cook other side, until puffed and lightly browned. Drain on absorbent paper. Repeat with remaining pappadams.

To microwave: Place 4 pappadams at a time on large plate, slightly overlapping edges, cook on HIGH for about 1 minute or until puffed on 1 side; turn over and cook further 1 minute or until puffed all over.

Makes 20.

FRESH FRUIT WITH GINGER YOGHURT SAUCE

Prepare fruit just before serving. Sauce can be made several hours ahead; keep, covered, in refrigerator. Recipe unsuitable to freeze.

1 medium peach, sliced
2 medium apples, sliced
1 medium pear, sliced
1 medium mango, sliced
3 medium bananas, sliced
250g punnet strawberries
2 medium oranges, segmented
GINGER YOGHURT SAUCE
2 cups plain yoghurt
2 tablespoons sugar
1 teaspoon grated orange rind
1 teaspoon grated fresh ginger
1 teaspoon chopped glacé ginger
Arrange fruit on serving platter. Serve with sauce.

Ginger Yoghurt Sauce: Combine all ingredients in a small bowl, mix well.

BERRY COCONUT TRIFLE

Trifle can be made a day ahead; keep, covered, in refrigerator. Decorate just before serving. This recipe is unsuitable to freeze.

350g packaged madeira cake
¼ cup orange juice
250g punnet strawberries
200g punnet raspberries
½ cup sugar
2 tablespoons arrowroot
1 cup water
3 cups (270g) coconut
1 cup icing sugar
1¼ litres (5 cups) milk
⅓ cup cornflour
300ml carton cream
1 tablespoon rosewater
Cut cake into 3cm cubes, arrange over base of serving dish (12 cup capacity). Sprinkle cake with orange juice. Blend or process berries until smooth, strain. Combine berry purée with sugar in medium saucepan, stir over high heat without boiling until sugar is dissolved.

Blend arrowroot with water, stir into berry mixture, stir over high heat for about 2 minutes (or microwave on HIGH for about 4 minutes) or until mixture boils and thickens. Remove from heat, cool to room temperature, pour over cake, refrigerate until firm.

Combine coconut, icing sugar and milk in large saucepan, cook over low heat for about 15 minutes, stirring occasionally (or microwave on HIGH for about 8 minutes). Strain mixture into large saucepan, discard coconut. Blend cornflour with cream, stir into milk mixture, stir over high heat (or microwave on HIGH for about 3 minutes) until mixture boils and thickens, cool to room temperature.

Stir rosewater into milk mixture, pour over berry layer, refrigerate for several hours or until firm. Decorate trifle with extra cream, strawberries and toasted flaked coconut, if desired.

Berry Coconut Trifle served with Fresh Fruit with Ginger Yoghurt Sauce.

Plate and board: The Country Trader

Make Your Own Essentials

Here we show you how to make yoghurt, soy milk, cottage cheese, peanut butter and mayonnaise, and grow bean sprouts, letting you have supplies as fresh as you want just when you want them. They can all be used in place of commercial varieties suggested in our recipes, if you prefer.

YOGHURT

You need to buy very fresh yoghurt to use as a starter for this recipe. The time it takes to thicken varies depending on the freshness of the starter and the temperature of the mixture and the room. Yoghurt makers are available; they take the guesswork out of the process. Yoghurt can be kept in refrigerator for up to 2 weeks. This recipe is unsuitable to freeze or microwave.

2½ cups milk
¼ cup full-cream milk powder
2 tablespoons plain yoghurt

STEP 1
Combine milk and powdered milk in medium bowl, whisk well until smooth.

STEP 2
Pour into saucepan, bring just to the boil, stirring. Remove from heat, cool to just above lukewarm (50°C).

STEP 3
Place yoghurt in medium bowl, gradually whisk in warm milk. Liquid should be lukewarm (41°C). Strain the liquid.

STEP 4
Pour mixture into 2 clean, warm jars, seal and place in warm position (about 30°C) for 10 hours, without moving; refrigerate mixture for several hours before serving.

Clockwise from top left: Soy Milk; Yoghurt; Cottage Cheese; Peanut Butter; Mayonnaise; Bean Sprouts.

SOY MILK

Sweeten milk with sugar or honey, if desired. Recipe can be made 10 days ahead; keep, covered, in refrigerator. Milk can be frozen for 2 months.

⅔ cup (125g) dried soy beans
1 litre (4 cups) warm water

STEP 1
Wash beans, place in large bowl, cover with water, cover, stand overnight; drain. Rinse beans under cold water, drain. Rub off skins with fingertips, discard skins.

STEP 2
Blend or process beans until they are finely ground.

STEP 3
Spoon mixture into a fine cloth, tie securely with string. Place cloth into large bowl, cover with the water, squeeze and press for 10 minutes. Remove from bowl, squeeze with hands to remove all liquid. Serve hot or cold.
     Makes 1 litre (4 cups).

COTTAGE CHEESE

Cheese can be made a week ahead; keep, covered, in refrigerator. This recipe makes about 1 cup (250g) cheese. This recipe is not suitable to freeze or microwave.

2 litres (8 cups) milk
2 tablespoons sour light cream

STEP 1
Heat milk in large saucepan until lukewarm. Place sour cream in large bowl, gradually stir in milk, cover, stand at room temperature overnight or until mixture is thick. Stand bowl in large bowl or dish containing enough warm water to come up to the level of the milk mixture, stand for about 1 hour or until the curd clots, replacing about 2 cupfuls of the water with hot water every 10 to 15 minutes so that the water remains warm. Occasionally spoon the more solid curd from the outside of the bowl to the centre to ensure that the curd clots evenly.

STEP 2
Drop a piece of cheesecloth or muslin into saucepan of boiling water; boil for 2 minutes, wring out, spread cloth over the top of large bowl, spoon curd into centre. Gather cloth corners together, secure with string. Suspend the curd above medium bowl, drain for 1 hour.

STEP 3
Remove curd from cloth, spoon curd into small bowl, cover, refrigerate before using.

SPROUTING SEEDS

Many varieties of seeds for sprouting are available from health food stores, as are sprouter kits for growing them. However, sprouts grow well if you follow the simple method described here. Sprouts keep for about a week in refrigerator after they are removed from their growing area.

STEP 1
Sprinkle 1 tablespoon seeds into a glass jar.

STEP 2
Cover seeds with warm water. Cover opening of jar with tulle or fine net, secure with elastic band. Invert jar to drain away water, place jar on side. Rinse and drain twice a day until sprouts have grown to desired size.

STEP 3
Sprouts are usually ready to eat in 3 to 6 days.

PEANUT BUTTER

Peanut butter can be kept in refrigerator for up to 2 months. Recipe unsuitable to freeze.

250g shelled, roasted, unsalted peanuts
1 tablespoon oil

STEP 1

Combine all ingredients in blender or processor, blend or process until as smooth as desired. Refrigerate.
　Makes 1 cup.

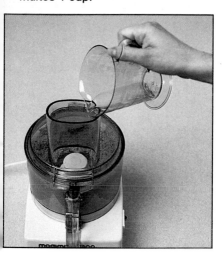

MAYONNAISE

Mayonnaise is easy to make; the main problem is usually curdling, which occurs when oil is added too quickly.

　If this happens, remove the curdled mixture from the blender or processor to a jug. Place another egg yolk into the blender or processor, add the curdled mixture drop by drop while the motor is operating. Once the mixture is holding together, add the rest of the curdled mixture in a thin stream while the motor is operating.

　Mayonnaise will keep for up to a week, covered, in refrigerator. This recipe is not suitable to freeze.

2 egg yolks
1 teaspoon dry mustard
2 teaspoons lemon juice
1 cup oil
2 tablespoons hot water, approximately

STEP 1

Blend or process egg yolks, mustard and juice until smooth. Add oil gradually in a thin stream while motor is operating.

STEP 2

Transfer mayonnaise to medium bowl; mayonnaise should be a thick consistency as shown. Stir in a little hot water for a thinner consistency.
　Makes about 1½ cups.

Glossary

Here are some names, terms and alternatives to help everyone use and understand our recipes perfectly.

ARROWROOT: is made from a combination of starchy extracts from the roots of various tropical plants; it is used mostly for thickening. Cornflour can be substituted.
BLACK-EYED BEANS: also known as black-eyed peas.
BREADCRUMBS:
Stale: use 1 or 2 day old white bread made into crumbs by grating, blending or processing.
Packaged: use commercially packaged breadcrumbs.
BROAD BEANS (fava beans): available fresh, frozen and dried.
BUCKWHEAT FLOUR: flour milled from buckwheat.
BURGHUL: cracked wheat.
BUTTER: we used sweet (salted) or unsalted butter in our recipes; 125g butter is equal to 1 stick butter.
BUTTERMILK: the liquid left from cream after separation; slightly sour in taste. Substitute skim milk, if preferred.

TOP ROW: From left: Polenta; Cracked Wheat; Rolled Rice.
BOTTOM ROW: From left: Hulled Millet; Couscous; Millet Meal.

CAROB: available in 50g and 75g blocks and in powdered form from health food shops.

CHEESE

Feta: a fresh, soft Greek cheese with a crumbly texture and a sharp, salty flavour. We used cheese with 15 per cent fat content.

Parmesan: sharp-tasting cheese used as a flavour accent. We used cheese with 30 per cent fat content.

Tasty: use a firm, good-tasting cheddar. We used cheese with 33 per cent fat content.

CHESTNUT SPREAD: purée of sweetened, flavoured chestnuts.

CHICK PEAS: cover dried peas well with water, stand overnight. Next day, drain, then boil in plenty of water until beans are tender for around 1 hour.

CHILLI POWDER: the Asian variety of the powder is the hottest and is made from ground chillies; it can be used as a substitute for fresh chillies in the proportion of ½ teaspoon ground chilli powder to 1 medium chopped chilli.

CIDER VINEGAR: made from unprocessed apple cider.

CINNAMON: can be bought in dried quills (sticks) or ground form. It is used in sweet and savoury recipes.

COCONUT: we used pre-packaged shredded, flaked and desiccated coconut in our recipes.

COCONUT CREAM/MILK: we used both canned coconut cream and milk; one can be substituted for the other. As a rule, the cream is thicker than the milk, but different brands vary. Coconut cream is also available in 200g cartons and 200g blocks of pure creamed coconut.

CORNFLOUR: cornstarch.

COUSCOUS: a fine cereal made from semolina.

CRACKED WHEAT: wheat which has been cracked by boiling, then re-dried; it is most often used in Middle Eastern cooking.

BELOW: From left: Soft Tofu; Firm Tofu; Tempeh.

CURRY POWDER: consists of a mixture of coriander, chilli, cumin, fennel, fenugreek and turmeric in varying proportions.

DASHI: is a basic fish and seaweed stock responsible for the distinctive flavour of Japanese food. It is made from dried bonito flakes and konbu. Instant dashi, a good substitute, is readily available. Dashi is used as a stock, soup or as an ingredient in dipping sauces.

DRIED GOURD: is a white vegetable marrow dried in strips. Available from Japanese specialty stores.

EGGPLANT: aubergine.

FENNEL: celery-like shoot has delicate, feathery leaves and slight aniseed flavour. Can be used either cooked or raw.

FLOURS

We have used several kinds of flour in this book. One cannot be substituted for another and give the same result as the picture. In a lot of recipes we have some white and wholemeal flour together; this is done to improve the texture of the cake or bread, etc.

ABOVE: Dried Gourd.

BELOW: From top: Shredded Coconut; Flaked Coconut; Desiccated Coconut.
RIGHT: From left: English Spinach; Silverbeet.

Rye flour: is made from ground rye and is low in gluten content.

White plain flour: all purpose flour.

Wholemeal plain flour: wholewheat flour; wholemeal flour without the addition of baking powder.

White self-raising flour: substitute white plain (all purpose) flour and baking powder in the proportion of ¾ metric cup plain flour to 2 level metric teaspoons baking powder, sift together several times before using. If using an 8oz measuring cup, use 1 cup white plain flour to 2 level metric teaspoons baking powder.

Wholemeal self-raising flour: wholewheat self-raising flour; add baking powder as above to make wholemeal self-raising flour.

GARAM MASALA: varied combinations of cardamom, cinnamon, cloves, coriander, cumin and nutmeg make this spice which is often used in Indian cooking. Sometimes pepper is used to make a hot variation. Garam masala is available in jars from Asian food stores and specialty stores.

GARBANZOS: canned chick peas; they should be drained, washed in running water then drained again.

GHEE: clarified butter.

GINGER

Fresh (green or root): scrape away outside skin and it is ready to grate, chop or slice as required.

Glacé: crystallised ginger can be substituted. Rinse off sugar with warm

water; dry ginger well before using.
Red pickled: is dyed and preserved in rice wine and sugar.
GREEN SHALLOTS: known as spring onions in some Australian States; scallions in some other countries.
GROUND ALMONDS: we used packaged, commercially-ground almonds in our recipes unless otherwise specified.
GROUND CORIANDER: seeds of the coriander (or cilantro) plant, which are dried then ground. It is the main ingredient in curry powder.
HAWAIIAN MIX: a combination of finely chopped sultanas, raisins, banana chips, dried papaw, pineapple and coconut. Available from health food stores.

HERBS: we have specified when to use fresh or dried herbs. We used dried (not ground) herbs in proportion of 1:4 for fresh herbs; for example, 1 teaspoon dried herbs instead of 4 teaspoons (1 tablespoon) chopped fresh herbs.
HOISIN SAUCE: is a thick sweet Chinese barbecue sauce made from salted black beans, onions and garlic.
HULLED MILLET: millet without husks.
KIWI FRUIT (Chinese gooseberry): fruit with hairy skin and soft, sweet green-coloured flesh.
KUMARA: is an orange-coloured sweet potato.

LAVASH: flat unleavened bread of Mediterranean origin.
LENTILS: there are many different types; all require overnight soaking before cooking with the exception of red lentils which are ready for cooking without soaking.
MILLET MEAL: coarsely ground millet.
MUSTARD
Seeded: French-style mustard with crushed seeds.
Dry: available in powder form.
French: smooth paste with sweet-sour taste.
OIL: we used a light polyunsaturated salad oil in our recipes unless otherwise specified. Use the oil of your choice.
OLIVE OIL: virgin oil is obtained only from the pulp of high-grade fruit. Pure olive oil is pressed from the pulp and kernels of second grade olives.
OYSTER MUSHROOMS: also known as abalone mushrooms; are small, fresh cultivated mushrooms.
PASTA SAUCE: commercially bottled Italian-style tomato sauce, usually eaten with pasta.
PEARL BARLEY: barley which has had most of its outer husk removed.
PEPPERS (capsicums): sweet or bell peppers.
PIMIENTOS: sweet red peppers preserved in brine in cans or jars.
PIMENTO (allspice): pimento is the

BELOW: Clockwise from left: Red Pickled Ginger; Fresh Ginger Root; Grated Fresh Ginger.

ABOVE: Oyster Mushrooms.

ABOVE: Clockwise from top left: Icing Sugar; Crystal Sugar; Raw Sugar; Castor Sugar; Brown Sugar. LEFT: Clockwise from left: Alfalfa Sprouts; Mung Bean Sprouts; Lentil Sprouts.

whole fruit; allspice is the ground form, used mostly in savoury recipes.
POLENTA: also known as cornmeal or maizemeal; is a type of meal ground from Indian corn.
RED SPANISH ONION: large red onion.
RICE: can be brown or white. Long grain rice is the most commonly used variety; it is hulled and polished. Brown rice is the natural whole grain before it has been processed; takes longer to cook than white rice.
ROSEWATER: extract of rose petals used to flavour sweet dishes, creams and cakes.
SNOW PEAS: (also known as mange-tout, sugar peas or Chinese peas); are small flat pods with tiny barely formed peas inside; they are eaten whole, pod and all. Snow peas do need to be topped and tailed; the older ones also need stringing. They require only a short cooking time either by stir-frying or blanching.
SOY SAUCE: made from fermented soy beans; we used the light and dark varieties. The light is generally used with white meat dishes, and the darker variety with red meat dishes. The dark is normally used for colour and the light for flavour.

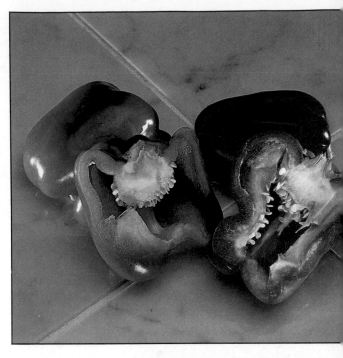

SPAGHETTI SQUASH: type of short vegetable marrow. The flesh resembles spaghetti when cooked.
SPINACH: we used flat-leafed English spinach or the darker spinach, also known as silverbeet.
SPROUTS: we used mostly mung bean sprouts or alfalfa sprouts. Sprout mixtures or salads are available, if you prefer.
SUGAR
We used coarse granulated table sugar also known as crystal sugar unless otherwise specified.
Castor: fine granulated table sugar.
Icing: confectioners' or powdered sugar. We used icing sugar mixture (not pure) in the recipes in this book.
Raw sugar: Natural light brown

ABOVE LEFT: From left: Sesame Seeds; Tahini Paste.
ABOVE RIGHT: Green and Red Peppers.

granulated sugar or ''sugar in the raw'' can be used.
SULTANAS: seedless white raisins.
TABASCO SAUCE: made with vinegar, hot red peppers and salt.
TAHINI: a paste made from sesame seeds. Available from health food stores and specialty shops.
TAMARI SHOYU: a thick, dark soy sauce made mainly from soy beans, without the wheat (used in standard soy sauce). It is used in dishes where the flavour of soy is important, such as dipping sauces and marinades (Shoyu is Japanese for soy.)

TEMPEH: is produced by a natural culture of soy beans; has a chunky, chewy texture.
TERIYAKI SAUCE: is based on the lighter Japanese soy sauce; it also contains sugar, spices and vinegar.
TOFU: made from boiled, crushed soy beans to give a type of milk. A coagulant is added, much like the process of cheese making. We used soft tofu and firm tofu. Tofu is easily digested, nutritious and has a slightly nutty flavour. Buy it as fresh as possible; keep any leftover tofu in the refrigerator under water, which must be changed daily.
TOFU SQUARES: available in packets from Japanese specialty stores.
TOMATO PASTE: a concentrated tomato purée used in flavouring soups, stews, sauces, etc.
TOMATO PUREE: is canned, puréed tomatoes (not tomato paste). Use fresh, peeled, puréed tomatoes as a substitute, if preferred.
TOMATO SAUCE: tomato purée in some countries.
VECON: is a natural vegetable stock paste available in health food stores.
VEGETABLE STOCK CUBE: contains no animal products but is salty to taste; 1 cube is equivalent to 2 teaspoons powdered bouillon.
VERMICELLI: thin, clear rice noodles.
WITLOF: also known as chicory or Belgian endive.
YEAST: compressed (fresh) yeast is available from health food stores; 3 level teaspoons dried yeast is equivalent to 30g compressed yeast.
ZUCCHINI: courgette.

LEFT: Clockwise from top left: Eggplant; Kumara; Zucchini; Green Shallots; Snow Peas.

Index

QUICK CONVERSION GUIDE

Wherever you live in the world you can use our recipes with the help of our easy-to-follow conversions for all your cooking needs. These conversions are approximate only. The difference between the exact and approximate conversions of liquid and dry measures amounts to only a teaspoon or two, and will not make any difference to your cooking results.

MEASURING EQUIPMENT

The difference between measuring cups internationally is minimal within 2 or 3 teaspoons' difference. (For the record, 1 Australian metric measuring cup will hold approximately 250ml.) The most accurate way of measuring dry ingredients is to weigh them. When measuring liquids use a clear glass or plastic jug with metric markings.

In this book we use metric measuring cups and spoons approved by Standards Australia.
- a graduated set of four cups for measuring dry ingredients; the sizes are marked on the cups.
- a graduated set of four spoons for measuring dry and liquid ingredients; the amounts are marked on the spoons.
- 1 TEASPOON: 5ml.
- 1 TABLESPOON: 20ml.

NOTE: NZ, CANADA, USA AND UK ALL USE 15ml TABLESPOONS. ALL CUP AND SPOON MEASUREMENTS ARE LEVEL.

DRY MEASURES

METRIC	IMPERIAL
15g	½oz
30g	1oz
60g	2oz
90g	3oz
125g	4oz (¼lb)
155g	5oz
185g	6oz
220g	7oz
250g	8oz (½lb)
280g	9oz
315g	10oz
345g	11oz
375g	12oz (¾lb)
410g	13oz
440g	14oz
470g	15oz
500g	16oz (1lb)
750g	24oz (1½lb)
1kg	32oz (2lb)

LIQUID MEASURES

METRIC	IMPERIAL
30ml	1 fluid oz
60ml	2 fluid oz
100ml	3 fluid oz
125ml	4 fluid oz
150ml	5 fluid oz (¼ pint/1 gill)
190ml	6 fluid oz
250ml	8 fluid oz
300ml	10 fluid oz (½ pint)
500ml	16 fluid oz
600ml	20 fluid oz (1 pint)
1000ml (1 litre)	1¾ pints

WE USE LARGE EGGS WITH AN AVERAGE WEIGHT OF 60g

HELPFUL MEASURES

METRIC	IMPERIAL
3mm	⅛in
6mm	¼in
1cm	½in
2cm	¾in
2.5cm	1in
5cm	2in
6cm	2½in
8cm	3in
10cm	4in
13cm	5in
15cm	6in
18cm	7in
20cm	8in
23cm	9in
25cm	10in
28cm	11in
30cm	12in (1ft)

HOW TO MEASURE

When using the graduated metric measuring cups, it is important to shake the dry ingredients loosely into the required cup. Do not tap the cup on the bench, or pack the ingredients into the cup unless otherwise directed. Level top of cup with knife. When using graduated metric measuring spoons, level top of spoon with knife. When measuring liquids in the jug, place jug on flat surface, check for accuracy at eye level.

OVEN TEMPERATURES

These oven temperatures are only a guide; we've given you the lower degree of heat. Always check the manufacturer's manual.

	C° (Celsius)	F° (Fahrenheit)	Gas Mark
Very slow	120	250	1
Slow	150	300	2
Moderately slow	160	325	3
Moderate	180	350	4
Moderately hot	190	375	5
Hot	200	400	6
Very hot	230	450	7